D0595855

I Love My Dog, But...

Avon Books are available at special quantity discounts for bulk purchases for sales promotions, premiums, fund raising or educational use. Special books, or book excerpts, can also be created to fit specific needs.

For details write or telephone the office of the Director of Special Markets, Avon Books, Inc., Dept. FP, 1350 Avenue of the Americas, New York, New York 10019, 1-800-238-0658.

I Love My Dog, But...

The Ultimate Guide to Managing Your Dog's Misbehavior

JOY TIZ, M.S., J.D.

AVON BOOKS ◆ NEW YORK

In loving memory of Cassius
1991–1995
The best friend I could ever have wanted

And Jet
1989–1997
My teacher, my friend

AVON BOOKS, INC.
1350 Avenue of the Americas
New York, New York 10019

Copyright © 1999 by Joy Tiz
Cover photograph by Bob Firth/International Stock
Interior design by Kellan Peck
Published by arrangement with the author
Library of Congress Catalog Card Number: 99-94875
ISBN: 0-380-78801-2
www.avonbooks.com

All rights reserved, which includes the right to reproduce this book or portions thereof in any form whatsoever except as provided by the U.S. Copyright Law. For information address Avon Books, Inc.

First Avon Books Trade Paperback Printing: September 1999

AVON TRADEMARK REG. U.S. PAT. OFF. AND IN OTHER COUNTRIES, MARCA REGISTRADA, HECHO EN U.S.A.

Printed in the U.S.A.

OPM   10   9   8   7   6   5   4   3   2   1

If you purchased this book without a cover, you should be aware that this book is stolen property. It was reported as "unsold and destroyed" to the publisher, and neither the author nor the publisher has received any payment for this "stripped book."

Contents

Introduction

It starts with a dream. Your dog. Visions of your faithful companion napping in front of the fireplace. Or maybe a precious little ball of fur romping with the kids.

So how come it all goes haywire? The precious furball gnawing the new carpet. Your faithful companion hopping the fence to explore neighborhood trash cans. Dogs biting the owners they're supposed to love.

The number of dogs relinquished to shelters every year is staggering. The number abandoned is astronomical. That's the bad news. The good news is, it *can* work. You can have the dog you want, the best friend you ever wanted. It just takes a little work.

A DOG ISN'T REALLY A DOG

The first step is to recognize that dogs don't think the way we do. Emotionally, they have a range of feelings that is remarkably similar to ours. When you say your dog loves you, you are absolutely right. Dogs do love their human companions. That's why we choose them as pets. But their minds work differently.

Domestic dogs didn't always exist. These animals started out as wild wolves, and in time humans discovered their usefulness. For example, their superior scenting and hearing abilities enabled them to detect the presence of potential food long before our human ancestors could. Eventually, they were bred selectively for the various skills that humans valued. Our ancestors no doubt also discovered that wolves were naturally suspicious of strangers. This useful trait is alive today in our domestic dogs. Your dog expresses it each time she barks at an unfamiliar noise.

The domestication started probably ten thousand years ago. Through the process of domestication, we have our pet dogs. Dogs, unlike wild wolves, can accept humans as fellow pack members. What's important to understand is that we did *not* breed out many wolf traits. The dog's high pack drive, for example, remains intact. It's a useful trait, as it keeps our dogs loyal and enables them to bond with us.

The dog/wolf connection has been confirmed scientifically through DNA testing. This technology has become important in wolf protection and reintroduction efforts. To enforce fines for killing a wild wolf in a protected area, officials must confirm that the animal was indeed a wild wolf and not a dog-wolf hybrid. Also, wolves are often moved to more favorable habitats. If the animal is a hybrid its chance of survival in the wild is virtually nil. However, in his 1995 book *In the Company of Wolves*, Peter Steinhart asserts that there is no DNA test that can distinguish a wild wolf from a domestic dog. He reports that dogs were bred out of wolf lines less than twenty thousand years ago, and genetically the two have not diverged much. This revelation has profound implications for dog owners. The relationship between a wolf and a domestic dog remains very close.

Have you ever seen your dog "kill" a pillow or toy? Watch as he shakes the life out of it and tears it to shreds. That's natural predatory behavior inherited directly from his wolf relatives. So is the irresistible urge to chase anything that moves. Rent a good documentary about wolves. Watch the way they interact; notice especially the ears and tails. Do you see anything familiar? Don't they look an awful lot like your dog in action? If you have more than one dog, it will be even more evident.

Some of our domestic dog breeds are so wolflike in appearance, they get to play wolves on TV and in the movies. Alaskan malamutes are frequent stand-ins for wild wolves.

So, what does all this have to do with getting your dog to quit pooping in the house? Everything. Having a wonderful canine companion requires understanding how your dog thinks and feels, and learning how to communicate your wishes. Although your dog has a gift for understanding how you *feel*, your thought processes are a complete mystery to him. Fortunately, you can learn to communicate with your dog in ways that make sense to the dog.

Understanding pack behavior is crucial to having a well-adjusted dog. Every wolf pack has an Alpha—a sort of CEO of the pack. A wolf pack is not a democracy, it's a dictatorship of the most benevolent sort. The Alpha has awesome responsibility: keeping order among the pack members and directing hunting activity. Only the fittest and brightest wolves gain Alpha status.

Every dog needs an Alpha. The Monks of New Skete, in their excellent books, talk about every dog's *right* to stewardship and leadership. That's what your dog needs from you.

Most canine behavior problems are the result of a faulty dog/owner bond. What's happened is that the owner hasn't established Alpha status with the dog. The dog may consider the owner a social equal, and pack rules dictate that a dog has an absolute right to ignore social equals. So the dog's behavior isn't really improper at all. It's entirely consistent with the Pack Code.

What it breaks down to for the dog is *trust*. A strong Alpha inspires trust in the dog. The dog is assured safety in the pack, the food will come, the beloved owner will return. Wolves adore the Alpha in their pack. Instinctively, they know their survival depends on the Alpha's skills. The domestic dog is no different. The absence of trust leads to extreme tension and anxiety in our dogs. Some dogs will act out this tension by testing limits, quite literally checking to see if you are an Alpha who can be counted on. Some seem to cave inward, reducing their anxiety by gnawing on anything they can, or by running away. Taken to its extreme, this tension causes some dogs to bite their owners.

We humans often, with the best intentions, make matters worse. We do it by humanizing our dogs. The owner who says she would never take her dog to obedience school because at school they boss the dogs around and make them do things they don't want to do is humanizing the dog. She misunderstands the dog's long heritage of utility, of being bred to serve humans. And she misunderstands the dog's need to identify an Alpha figure. The owner who thinks it is horrible to put a dog in a crate knows *he* would hate being in a crate, and incorrectly assumes his dog would, too. He's failing to understand that dogs, like wolves, are den animals. Dogs naturally seek out snug, cozy spots for snoozing. Does your dog like to curl up in a corner or under a table for a nap? That's the denning instinct. Dogs actually appreciate a cozy den of their own.

An experienced trainer recently told me why she uses food treats in her training classes. "I see it as a reward for a job well done," she insisted. Well, who cares how the *human* sees it? We need to focus on how the *dog* sees it. Treat-training produces quick but cheap results. Let's hope the owner has a fanny pack full of treats the day someone accidentally leaves a gate open and she has to issue a panic stay command. Treat-training makes for good PR. Anxious owners don't have to be firm or scold the dog properly.

In a pack, a subordinate wolf will sometimes offer up food to a higher ranking wolf. It's a gesture of *appeasement*. The wolf or dog is saying, "Yes, yes! You outrank me! Here, take the food. Just don't hurt me, please!" Imagine how a dominant dog must perceive an owner offering up biscuits to elicit a sit. In effect, the dog has trained the owner to deliver tidbits on command. An Alpha does not bribe subordinates into good behavior. An Alpha commands respect, just by being an Alpha. A dog will do what you ask because his greatest joy in life is pleasing the beloved Alpha. Why would we want to tamper with that? You need a food treat to teach a chicken to play the piano but not to teach a dog to sit. Appreciate that.

We often put a lot of energy into getting our dogs to *like* us. Don't worry, your dog likes you. She loves you. It may not be the same quality of deep and abiding respect she'll feel for you when you become Alpha, but it's safe to say that your dog likes you just fine. To ensure that our dogs like us, we tend to do things that would make *humans* like us. We offer up food. We don't criticize. We don't make demands. See, we're nice owners.

We give lots of chewies and toys. The problem is, this stuff doesn't work on dogs. They're the original opportunists, however, and they'll do nothing to discourage you from giving them what they want. But it won't make for a happier dog. Invariably, at the beginning of a new obedience class, owners will say the dog really likes the spouse, or child, or some other relative best. A few weeks of working with the dog, and the same owners will report that the dog has shifted alliances: "She only listens to me" or "She follows me everywhere now." No surprise.

Obedience work is an excellent way to improve your relationship with your dog. It gives you the chance to become an Alpha. It gives the dog a job. Remember, we domesticated them in the first place to be of service to us. A dog needs a job. Ever see a Border collie at a herding trial? Pure canine ecstasy. The dog is getting a chance to do what he was put on the planet to do. Your dog learns to please you, in ways that are in the best interests of both. Obedience training has even made for a longer life for many dogs. A dog properly educated to an airtight stay is a controllable dog. It's wonderful to issue the command "Come!" to your dog and have her obey it. The dog's desire to earn your praise can outweigh the fascination of a passing cat or other distraction. It just takes work. And patience. And a sense of humor.

Owners often report that some behavior problems drop off after a few weeks of obedience work. From the dog's perspective, this makes perfect sense. The dog has a lot to think about, a job to do. His anxiety levels are going down. He begins to recognize his Alpha. He feels more trusting and more secure. There's less need and less point in testing limits. A dog will contentedly assume his position in the pack, if that position is made clear.

Obedience school is an excellent place to start working on your relationship with your dog. All dogs need to go to school. It's not the magic cure-all for all dog/owner problems, but, it's a great start. Developing the right kind of relationship with your dog requires a lifestyle change. It requires opening your mind and accepting that your dog sees things differently than you do. It takes some discipline to stop thinking of your dog as a human child and start thinking of him as a wolf who has graciously accepted you as a fellow pack member.

THE DOG LOG

The Dog Log is your own private journal. Throughout this book, you will find written homework assignments to go in your log. If you complete the assignments, you will find yourself learning a great deal about your canine friend. As a result, your ability to communicate with each other will improve dramatically.

If the dog's behavior has been making you really crazy, or if there is conflict among household members about the dog, the Dog Log is a safe place to express your feelings, both positive and negative. Don't hold back! You need not share it with anyone.

The Dog Log is a powerful tool for understanding your dog's behavior. That understanding will make it much, much easier for you to change the dog's behavior and settle in to a much happier, healthier dog/owner relationship.

 HOMEWORK ASSIGNMENT:
Starting Your Dog Log

You'll need a Dog Log for your homework assignments. Don't worry about format or penmanship.

First Assignment

Write down the behaviors your dog engages in that you would like to change. The next time you observe one, write it down and include the date. Also include some notes about what *else* was going on at the time.

Once the canine crime is on paper, you will start to see some interesting connections.

Example: Fluffy chewed up the new throw rug in the living room while I was at work.
What else was going on: My husband left on a business trip this morning. We were very rushed and he almost missed the plane.

We can already start to formulate some ideas on what happened with Fluffy. Perhaps the rushed good-bye scene made her anxious.

The idea of the Dog Log is to help you understand what environmental influences may be affecting your dog. Try to have fun with it, too.

For this assignment, keep track of your dog's problem behaviors for one week. Then go back and review your notes. What you're looking for are patterns; you'll probably find that your dog is far more consistent than you imagined. What behaviors could be based in anxiety? What may have caused the anxiety? For example, one owner discovered that her dog was destructive only when left alone during the morning hours. When he was left for the evening, the house was still in one piece. The owner did some sleuthing and found out that her neighbor was allowing her three dogs out every morning to roam loose through the neighborhood. The dogs usually returned within an hour or two and were then confined to the yard.

Three dogs romping about all over one's own front lawn is enough to send any dog into a frenzy. The owner was able to understand that her dog's behavior was driven by frustration, not "spite." She now can attempt to reason with the neighbor, contact animal control, or find a way to confine her dog securely until the marauding is over.

CHAPTER ONE

Puppy Love

Puppies are the most adorable creatures on earth. This is solid evidence of the Wisdom of Nature: their cuteness keeps us from strangling them. Puppies are actually miniature terrorists. They don't do as they're told, they run all over the place and have no respect for property rights.

You were probably thrilled when you brought New Puppy home. Everyone in the household was excited. Now you're having a hard time remembering what made this seem like such a good idea. Don't worry, all of this is perfectly normal. You're in Puppy Shock.

PUPPY SHOCK

Are you absolutely astonished at how much trouble a little puppy can create? Amazed at how much supervision he requires? You have probably lived with a dog before. It was not like this! Here's what happens: You had your previous dog for many years, maybe a lifetime. You got used to life with an adult dog. That's what you thought you were getting into.

If instead you are a novice dog owner, your previous experiences may have been with other people's well-behaved adult dogs. No wonder you're reeling. No one prepared you for the joys of puppyhood. The good news is, it doesn't last forever. You can get through it with all of your sanity and most of your belongings intact.

SURVIVAL GEAR

Before you read any further, *get a crate!* Until you do that, you won't be able to concentrate anyway. By crating the ball of fur, you can relax for a few moments without worrying that the little darling is about to gnaw through an electrical cord and flambé himself.

Yes, I have raised puppies without a crate. I don't remember any of it. Psychologists tell us we often block out traumatic memories. Crating will make your life much easier. Housebreaking will certainly be easier.

It is not cruel to crate a dog. Dogs, like wolves, are den animals. Have you ever noticed how dogs like to curl up and snooze in corners or under tables? That's the denning instinct at work. They naturally seek out secure, cozy spaces. You can readily crate-train a young puppy. Once that's done, she'll be easy to crate as an adult, should the need arise. If you decide to travel with your canine friend, you'll be very glad you started this early.

Training *you* is another matter. You must put the pup in the crate and ignore the yelps, howls, and whines. She is not dying. If you ignore the pup, she'll eventually wear herself out, realize this is not going to work, and take a nap. Fortunately, puppies need lots of naps. If you really cannot bear the sounds of her demands for attention, throw a sheet over the crate. Once it's dark, dogs usually flop down and go to sleep. Do not cave in on this! Puppies operate on the principle that any attention is better than no attention. If you run over to the crate to scold the puppy for making a fuss, you will quickly and effectively train the puppy to demand your attention. Many training books advise you to correct the puppy for making a racket in her crate. Big mistake. Getting no response from you is what teaches the puppy to accept crate time.

The crate should be large enough for the pup to stand up

and turn around in, but no larger. We'll talk more about that shortly.

The crate is for short intervals only. It's for those times when you can't supervise every move the puppy makes. At bedtime, move the crate into your bedroom. It will do wonders for the bonding process.

Invent a cute name for the crate. Refer to it as the puppy's "little house," or her "place," or something cute and creative. Why? You must avoid projecting any negative human feelings you may have about the crate. If you call it the "cage" or "prison," the pup is going to hear that meaning in your tone of voice. Canines are exquisitely sensitive to our voice inflections.

Feed the puppy in her crate. At nap time, let her have a toy or chewy in it. You want to create happy associations with her snug, cozy, secure little den. Resistant owners are often amazed when the puppy starts putting herself in the crate. Puppies will often do this when they are really tired and need a good, uninterrupted nap.

NO-NO'S FOR OWNERS

Take all of your newspapers to the nearest recycling facility. That way you won't be tempted to roll one up and swat the puppy with it. Actually, for a year or so, you should cancel newspaper delivery entirely. Old habits die hard. Although some puppies who were swatted with newspaper grow into stable adults anyway, this is nothing but sheer serendipity and good karma.

You know now that your puppy is a domesticated wolf at heart. A mama dog and her litter are a replica of an Alpha wolf with his pack. She maintains order using the same corrections a wolf in the wild uses. Your puppy hasn't been away from his mama very long. He knows she never swatted him with a newspaper. He also knows that when she corrected him, it worked. Therefore, you must model your corrections after the mama dog's. It's what the puppy understands. Growling, glaring, muzzle-grabbing, and a possible occasional scruff-shaking will get your point across. Rolled-up newspaper often produces aggression problems that surface during canine adolescence. And you can't really blame the puppy who was disciplined with a newspaper when he shreds every piece of paper in the house at the first opportunity.

Correcting a dog properly requires learning the techniques used by higher-ranking canines to discipline unruly subordinates. What's more important to learn is to develop the right attitude about corrections. That is the hard part. It does not come naturally for us.

THE LANGUAGE OF PUPPY LOVE

Your puppy does not understand your language. Accept this. Dog brains are not constructed in a way that allows them to communicate with words, although after enough repetition, a dog can learn to associate an object with a word, like *leash*. What your dog does understand perfectly well is his mother's language. He knows that a stern growl means he is in big, big trouble. Mama dogs correct quickly, and with a minimum of fuss. It's part technique and part attitude.

If you want a well-mannered pup, you have to learn to *growl*. You can use the word "NO!", but growl it out to a menacing, threatening "NOOOOO!" Or, if your pup is of German heritage, "AUUUUSSSSS!" Make it bloodcurdling. You must use your voice in a way that feels utterly ridiculous to you. It's not ridiculous to the pup.

Women, especially, have to work on voice control. Our voices are higher pitched and it's harder to deliver a really impressive growl. That high-pitched voice is the puppy's cue to tune you out. To a puppy's ears, much of our conversation sounds like *whining*. His littermates whined. So, using puppy logic, you must be a littermate. He knows he's allowed to ignore littermates; they're his social equals. Mama Dog, like an Alpha wolf, did not whine at her pups. Nor did she chase him around the den, pleading with him to knock off the puppy antics. Nope. She gave him her most menacing growl, along with a stern glare. It got through.

When you catch puppy gnawing on the forbidden, give him your best, most ferocious growl. At the least, the pup should stop what he's doing and look at you. Good! The second the gnawing stops, let the praise begin: "Goooood puppy!" Then remove the item.

STOP THE VIOLENCE

Please, never, ever hit your puppy. No matter how angry or frustrated you may get. Better to stick the puppy in the crate until you cool off. Use corrections that the pup can understand.

Some trainers continue to recommend a cuff under the chin for serious misbehavior. This technique can't really hurt an adult dog, but it doesn't work. Hitting makes no sense to a dog. His mother never hit him. When a dog is hit, he is stunned. He's so busy trying to decipher what just happened to him, the lesson itself is lost.

Hitting can backfire, with disastrous results. If a puppy is disciplined with hitting, he may cringe, cower, and run away. Eventually, as he matures, he is going to strike back. Again, don't blame the dog. When he bites, it's going to be out of legitimate self-defense.

Once you've learned to deliver proper Alpha-style corrections, you'll see spectacular results. And with none of the guilt and anxiety that hitting creates. Accept that with puppies it will take many repetitions before the lesson gets through. When it does, you'll not only have corrected a problem behavior, but earned your puppy's trust and respect.

THE PUPPY'S PLAY BITING

All puppies do this. All puppies must learn not to. Mouthing and nipping are perfectly acceptable littermate play, but you are not a littermate. No dog should be allowed even to entertain the idea that putting her mouth on a human is acceptable behavior. Play biting needs to be corrected sternly. Correct the puppy just the way her mama did. Grab that little muzzle and give it a squeeze while looking her in the eye and using your menacing growl. While holding the muzzle you may also introduce an important and effective command. In a stern voice say, "No Bites!" Don't be too quick to release the pup. You aren't going to injure her and she knows that.

Muzzle-grabbing is a strong display of dominance and authority. Fortunately, she is still little and you can do this easily. It is a powerful correction tool. It's also a difficult technique for humans to master. Often, the pup will give a little whimper while you're holding her muzzle. Owners fall apart over this. They think they've hurt the puppy. That isn't what happens. If the pup whimpers, she's offering up a show of submission and respect. Exactly what you want! When you release her, are her ears pinned back? Is her head held low? Congratulate yourself. You got through! She is not frightened of you. She is using canine body language to signal respect for your authority. She is apologizing for dissing you. Does she lick your hand? Or just gaze away for a few moments? Give her lots of gushing praise. She's learning valuable lessons.

Or does the pup instantly resume the mouthy stuff? You didn't get through that time. Do it again. Once the mouthing has become thoroughly entrenched, it can take many corrections to eliminate.

This powerful technique does require a good sense of timing and coordination. Some owners get into real wrestling matches with their pups, undermining their own authority. If you get the chance to observe a mama dog with her litter, you'll see this correction demonstrated flawlessly. Watch closely, though. Mama dog is quick. She isn't particularly tender when disciplining, either. It's all about real puppy love. Instinctively, the mama knows she must teach her pups to be led by an Alpha. It's how she ensures their survival. The pups don't like being disciplined, but they trust Mama. A mama dog would kill for her puppies or die for them in an instant. They know that. They don't resent her for asserting her authority. Nor does the mama feel guilt or anxiety about doing what must be done. She's the interim Alpha and it's part of her job.

Does your pup resist? Does she try to squiggle away, refusing eye contact? She's on her way to our Aggressive Dog Program, which will cost you a lot of money. She obviously cares nothing about your hard-earned cash, so correct her! And count your blessings that she's not a full-grown Doberman who still thinks play biting is good, clean fun.

Yes, you will probably have to correct this play biting business about fifty million times a day until the lesson sinks in. Or you can choose not to, and call me when you have a full-grown, snapping, biting, out-of-control terrorist on your hands.

Owners too often fail to take this mouthy behavior seriously. "Oh, she's only a puppy. She'll outgrow it," they insist. She's only a puppy, so we can still do something about it. When pups put their mouths on you, they are asserting *dominance* over you. Among littermates, this is how the pecking order is established. The puppy is testing you. Are you a littermate I can push around? She needs to know. It doesn't take much for the play biting to escalate into real biting. If it's allowed to continue, the dog will have no reservations about biting when she doesn't get her own way later on. Don't blame the dog.

CHEWING

This is yet another good reason why you got that crate. To a puppy, anything he can get his mouth on is a chewy. There's a good reason for this: he's teething, and it's uncomfortable. You will have to correct him each and every time he puts his mouth on a nonchewy, just as with the biting. Or be prepared to replace everything you own at least three times. By crating the pup when you can't supervise him closely, you make your job much easier. He won't develop as many bad habits in the first place. The most common mistake is giving the pup too much freedom. For now, he does not need the run of the entire house. Look at how little he is! Do not allow him in any room when you aren't there to supervise. Try to draft the rest of the household into service. Take turns on "puppy watch."

Another common mistake is providing too many chewies. We all do this when we get a new puppy. We rush out to the pet supply store and charge six hundred dollars' worth of toys and chewies. You're certainly free to do that. Just give them to the pup one or two at a time. If he has too many, he'll get confused. From his perspective, everything must be a chewy.

An ice cube makes a fine puppy chewy, by the way. It is also inexpensive. If you want to go all out, freeze some beef bouillon in the ice tray. The cold helps numb the teething pain.

Check with your vet about giving ice chewies to an adult dog,
though. It can be hard on the tooth enamel.

Many training manuals prescribe "stimulus substitution."
That is, when puppy gnaws on a chair leg, you scold and offer
a chewy. Don't fall for that. It confuses the pup and looks like
bribery. His mother did not bribe him. He can learn to tell the
difference between an authorized chewy and Everything Else
on the Planet. When he chews something forbidden, use your
best growl and glare. When he stops and looks up at you (if
you're growling properly, he will), PRAISE HIM. It's not enough
to scold bad behavior. You must praise him for the act of not
chewing. He'll get the idea much faster that way.

HOUSEBREAKING

Try not to be too anxious over housebreaking. It's really not that
difficult, once you learn to work with the pup's basic nature.
Here's where your crate really comes in handy. To the puppy,
it's a den. Wolf dens are kept immaculate. The first few days of
a dog or wolf puppy's life, Mama takes care of elimination.
She licks the babies to stimulate urination and defecation. She
promptly consumes all the waste products. This provides parasite
control and eliminates odors that would draw the attention of
predators. Once the pups discover locomotion, Mama starts
shoving them away from the sleeping and eating place for elimination. This is early housebreaking at its most efficient.

A conscientious breeder will do a great service to future
owners by keeping the puppy pen clean. A thorough scrubbing
ten to twelve times a day is average. By keeping the puppy pen
clean, the breeder helps the pups develop the urge to avoid their
own waste products.

That is why the size of the crate is important. If it's too big,
the puppy can eliminate and avoid having to lie in her own
mess. Thrift often dictates that you buy one crate per dog, so
many owners have crates that will accommodate the pup when
she is full grown. No problem. Just slip a board in the crate to
make puppy's space smaller for now.

Most puppies won't soil their Sacred Sleeping Space. That
is why you can't keep the pup crated for long periods. Puppies

need to eliminate after they eat, drink, nap, play, and about five hundred other times at random during the day. For a while, your life will be totally controlled by the pup's elimination schedule. If you observe the pup carefully, you will be able to identify the "potty dance" when you see it. It generally involves circling, sniffing, and whining. At the first sign of the potty dance, scoop her up and whisk her outside! Timing is crucial. You need excellent reflexes for this. Yes, you must watch the pup every second she is out of her crate. This should inspire you: EVERY TIME THE PUP GOES IN THE HOUSE, YOU ARE STARTING THE ENTIRE HOUSEBREAKING PRO-CESS OVER FROM THE BEGINNING. Do you really want that? Again, try to enlist other household members. But be certain they understand and accept the responsibility. Apparently, "Watch the puppy" can have more than one meaning. I once rescued a smart little golden retriever puppy. When I needed a nap, I asked my boyfriend to "watch the puppy" for me. When I woke up, I learned that his version of "watch" was to follow the puppy around with a rag and a bottle of carpet cleaner. Communication is everything.

Before bedtime, withhold food and water for three or four hours. Your final act before retiring will be taking puppy outside. You want to be certain she is really empty before she goes to bed for the night. Most pups can hold it until daylight, if you avoid overstimulating them before bed. No playing before beddy-bye! What if the pup wakes up at three A.M. and makes a big row? She may really need to go out. With very young pups (under twelve weeks), err on the side of caution and take them out. Some pups will make a game of this and demand to go out at all hours, just for the fun of it. Test the pup. Does she settle down after a few minutes, once she realizes she's not going anywhere?

In the morning, your first act must be a trip outside for the puppy. Buy one of those coffeemakers with a built-in timer.

There's a secret to getting housebreaking done in record time. Each and every time the pup goes outside, you go along. The first time she relieves herself out-of-doors, praise her to the skies! Here's where virtually everyone goes wrong. Do *not* make the mistake of praising the puppy as soon as she is finished.

YOU MUST PRAISE THE DOG EFFUSIVELY WHILE SHE IS PIDDLING. That's right, while she is in the process of relieving herself, you are standing there telling her in your most animated voice that she is the most wonderful puppy who ever lived. This does not come naturally for most humans. It violates our sense of propriety. But she's a dog. She does not see this process the way you do. If you make the mistake of waiting until she is finished, who knows what she'll think she's being praised for? A puppy's short-term memory and attention span are about equal to those of a gnat. If you don't praise her in the act, she won't get it. Once she does go outside, she'll also be drawn back to the same spot, due to the scent. If you have adult dogs, they can be a real help. Puppies copy adult dogs. And adult dogs leave lots of scent outside.

Yes, if your neighbors observe you, they will call County Mental Health. Imagine the sight of you in your bathrobe, during the eleven o'clock news, making an enormous fuss over a dog for peeing. So what? Ask them how long it took to get their dog housebroken. Be smug.

As you are whisking the pup outside (carry her, to reduce the risk of accidents), teach her the word you want to use for the act of going outdoors to eliminate. As you take her out, ask, "Outside?" in your animated happy voice. Eventually, she'll associate the word with going out to relieve herself. Look forward to her adulthood, when all you'll have to do is say "Outside?" and she'll run to the door. It'll happen. The most exciting day of your life will be when your puppy goes to the door and scratches because she needs to go out. Your wedding, the day you got the big promotion, the day you won the lottery, will all pale in comparison.

Paper Training

There's another reason you were advised to stop reading newspapers. That way you won't be tempted to paper-train your puppy. Unless you live on the 147th floor, there's no good reason for it. It doubles your workload. Once the puppy is paper-trained, she'll be so proud of herself she won't want to give it up. Then you'll have to make the transition from paper to outside. Lots of luck. A thoroughly paper-trained dog will spend fifteen hours in the park where ten billion dogs have eliminated and hold it until she gets home to her beloved paper. If you insist on paper-training, be prepared for Transition Day(s). Bring a sleeping bag. You'll have to keep the poor dog outside until her bladder is about to burst. If someone carelessly left an old newspaper lying on the ground, your whole day will be shot and you'll have to do it again.

Freudian Slips

It's amazing how many owners are willing to live with partially housebroken dogs. If the pup makes a mistake in the house, there is only one reason: he was not supervised properly. Don't go crazy over it. There is controversy about whether a scolding after the fact is fair and equitable. Some pups probably can make the connection if they are confronted with physical evidence. Please don't rub a dog's nose in it. It's a revolting idea, and does nothing to enlighten the pup.

The problem with after-the-fact corrections is that too often what the pup learns is to improve his concealment tactics. Rather than learning not to eliminate indoors, he learns that his owner gets angry if the mess is found. So the pup gets better at stealth pooping. So it's far better to prevent mishaps than to try to correct them later. It takes real diligence. But it doesn't last forever.

Toilet training shouldn't be traumatic for dog or owner (or trainer). When a client calls and gleefully reports that Puppycakes *only* had two accidents in the house this week, I know I have failed. I failed to communicate the concept of supervision. How could the puppy have had an accident? If he was being watched closely enough, it would be impossible.

What if you're doing everything right and it's not working? There are several possible explanations. Is the pup getting too much freedom? This is the most frequent cause of housebreaking problems. Tighten up the control. Keep the puppy on leash in the house if he's prone to scurrying away. It is hard work. But the worst should be over in about two weeks or so if you are truly diligent. Is another household member sabotaging you? Accept that the bulk of the task may fall on you and persevere.

The prevailing theory is that dogs will not eliminate in their crates. Usually it's true. Now and then, we find an exception. If your puppy has an accident in the crate, don't panic. There are a few things to check out. First, how long was the pup left in there? Two or three hours is quite reasonable. If you have a securely fenced yard, you can leave the pup there while you're at work. Do thoroughly check the yard first, though. Puppies can wriggle through amazingly small spaces. One client didn't believe me until he personally observed his thirty-pound puppy glide gracefully through the kitty door. If the pup is outside when you're not home, you won't have the opportunity to praise him when he eliminates out there. But the habit will be forming, and that's a good thing. If you don't have a secure yard, you'll have to get creative. Can you hire a responsible neighborhood kid to take the puppy out for you? Can someone in the household come home for lunch? Can you leave the puppy with someone who is home all day? You just can't leave a puppy crated for an entire day. It's cruel and it encourages soiling in the crate.

What about the crate itself? Is it too big? Can the puppy make a mess and escape it? Often, it's the stuff we put in the crate that creates problems. We humans always insist on putting a nice soft blankie, or at least newspaper, on the floor. Absorbent material just encourages the puppy to eliminate. The mess goes away. With a blanket, the pup can also get overheated.

Sometimes what's thwarting you are early puppyhood experiences. If the pup's breeder didn't keep the puppy pen spotless, the puppy may have developed the habit of lying around in his own mess. These pups are a challenge to housebreak: the natural motivation for staying clean isn't there to help you. But it can be done.

Bruno

Bruno's owners contacted me about puppy training. He was then ten weeks old, and was soon to be a very large dog. His owners were bright and insightful and quickly grasped the concept of crate training. There was only one problem: Bruno went potty in the crate. It didn't seem to faze him at all. He would flop right down in the mess and take a nap. Out of the crate, he seemed to have no control. He had been checked by a vet, so we knew we could rule out an organic cause.

During our initial interview, I learned that Bruno was spending his weekdays with friends. Sort of a puppy day care arrangement so he wouldn't have to be alone.

Bruno's owners were doing everything exactly right. They supervised him diligently in the house. But Bruno never did the potty dance, never gave any indication that he needed to eliminate. Eventually we discovered that the puppy-sitter was unwilling to supervise him every second he was out of the crate. So Bruno was learning that it is perfectly acceptable to potty in the house.

Also, Bruno had been purchased from a breeder who specialized in working ranch dogs. We surmised that the puppies had been left kenneled many hours each day while the breeder was tending to ranch chores, and cleanliness had not been maintained.

Bruno's owners were, understandably exasperated. Living with an enormous unhousebroken dog would be no fun. So Bruno was boarded with me. His owners referred to the arrangement as "puppy camp." My adult dogs were deputized as camp counselors. Their task was to educate by example. Observing their consistency in eliminating out-of-doors would be good for Bruno.

Bruno was a bright puppy, quite willing to please. But he was clearly not getting the hang of this housebreaking business. The solution? We had to create a new habit.

Because of his early experiences, it may never upset Bruno to eliminate indoors. Compare this to a thoroughly housebroken dog: If illness causes such a dog to have an accident, he is utterly mortified. In Bruno's case we would have to rely on repetition and reinforcement.

Unlike most puppies, Bruno had to be supervised closely while he was *in* his crate, as well as out of it. Bruno's life became very structured for the next four weeks. Every two hours, he was taken from crate to outside. Always the same spot. After eliminating, he could have supervised outdoor playtime. The lesson was: Go potty outside and you win some play time. Then back to the crate. Yes, this was a full-time operation. When I had to leave, he stayed in a fenced area with the Big Dogs. That way, he could get accustomed to eliminating outside. It was constant repetition. Crate to outside. Every two hours. By the third week, Bruno turned a corner. During his indoor playtime (he was kept on a leash, even then), he went to the front door. I took him out and he went right to his potty spot and did his business. His owners left him with me for one more week, to play it safe.

Happily, Bruno is now a housebroken dog. He didn't get off to the best possible start, but the job got done.

If you're having a lot of trouble with this chore, tighten up the regimen. Keep in mind, most puppies do instinctively seek to move away from the den to eliminate. Even if your pup missed this lesson, you can instill a new habit. It just takes lots of repetition, praise, and endless patience.

If you adopt an adult dog who isn't reliably housebroken, use the same procedures as those outlined for puppies. It generally takes less time, because the dog has better sphincter control and an attention span longer than a nanosecond.

PLAY!

Puppies like to spend all of their free time playing. Fortunately, they conk out from exhaustion frequently. Play is more than just a good time. It's an important part of the puppy's development. She needs to develop her nervous system, bones, and muscles this way. Most puppies seem to understand the importance of good play.

Play with your puppy. It's what they do best. Just avoid games that encourage that mouthing business. Roughhousing can get out of hand. And no tug-of-war games! It just encourages gangster traits. Remember, that's how littermates play. There's lots of play fighting among puppies. You can have fun without creating a terrorist. Teach your puppy to play fetch. Play hide-and-seek: have someone hide and call to the puppy from the hiding place. Hide-and-seek is mentally challenging as well as fun.

SLEEP

Your puppy needs lots of good, uninterrupted sleep. She knows when. Let her sleep. She really needs it if she is to grow into a healthy, stable adult. The puppy's need for sleep can be a problem with children around. They may overtire her. Luckily you have a crate: when she's tired, she can sleep there all snug and secure. Teach the children not to disturb her. Puppies often seek out their crates at naptime. When a puppy puts herself in her crate, she's hanging up a "Do Not Disturb" sign.

EARLY FORMAL EDUCATION: PUPPY HEAD START

Early puppyhood is the most teachable time of your dog's life. We're talking about pups under four months of age. They adore you. They want to listen. They love to please. They're a little insecure, so they tag along after you, often getting underfoot. The will to power isn't fully developed. They don't want to take over the whole world. Yet.

If your pup is younger than sixteen weeks, you have a real dilemma. You may see ads for "puppy kindergarten." It's a great idea. Unfortunately, the risk of deadly infectious diseases will never be higher. It's the worst possible time to expose your puppy to other dogs. Do not listen to any trainer who insists it's safe to bring your puppy to class. The one and only authority on this is your vet. The vet is in the best position to advise you as to when it's safe to take the little one out into the Big World. Your vet knows which diseases are most prevalent in your area and the efficacy of the various vaccines. The vet will put your puppy on a shot schedule. Adhere to this *religiously.* The cost of vaccinations is a pittance compared to the cost of a bout with parvovirus. Few puppies survive this virus. Your puppy received some early immunity from mother's milk, assuming the mother was properly vaccinated. That immunity wears off quickly. No one knows exactly when. Until it does, the puppy's shots won't "take." This is why the vet put your puppy on a schedule, for maximum protection. From the series, the pup will eventually develop good immunity.

Two weeks after I got my Thunder, his litter contracted parvo.

His little brothers and sisters became suddenly and violently ill. Several died in the car on the way to the vet. The breeder hadn't started them on their vaccinations. It was a cost-cutting measure. She lost all but one little male. Fortunately, my Thunder-puppy was spared. He's had lots of shots.

So if the vet says no contact with other dogs, or the outside world, that's the final word. Don't worry. There is plenty you can do to start educating your youngster. You can do your own in-home Puppy Head Start Program.

Make It Fun

Training for a young puppy should be fun. All fun. Make it a game. You'll condition the little squirt to consider training a good time. When he's a teenager, you'll be glad you did.

The overall agenda with the Puppy Head Start Program is to teach some basics and lay the foundation for good obedience work.

School Supplies

With most puppies, you can skip the chain collar. He needs to think of this as one big game. He's malleable at this age. You don't need harsh corrections. There are a few especially hardheaded, dominant pups who do better with a chain collar, but they are the exceptions. Get the pup a little buckle collar. Don't sink a lot of money into this. He'll outgrow it in about four days. Let him wear it around for a few days. With a very young puppy, start conditioning him for the leash by tying a short piece of clothesline to the buckle collar. Let him drag it around for a few hours, until he stops being afraid of it.

Good Manners

I don't care what any training manual says. If you want a happy life, the very first command your new puppy should learn is "Sit." "Sit" becomes the puppy's means of getting whatever she wants at the moment. She wants your attention? Fine. Have her sit. The humans are dining and it smells really interesting? Fine.

Make her sit nicely. She wants her ball to be tossed? Sounds like fun. Make her sit first. The puppy's entire life should revolve around sitting nicely. What you want to do is get it through her dogette brain that sitting nicely is the only hope she has of ever getting anything. Fortunately, puppies are opportunistic and they catch on quickly.

Teaching a puppy to sit is easy. Give her an authoritative "Sit!" and the hand signal. Do *not* repeat the sit command. Alphas do not negotiate. While she's learning, you will have to place her in the sit. The easiest way to place a puppy is to cup your hand under her little bottom and sort of scoop her into position. Once she is sitting, PRAISE HER. Use lots of gushing praise. Puppies are suckers for praise. Even if you had to put her in the sit, she gets the praise. Puppy wants a biscuit? Fine. Hold it up and do the scoop. She'll fall into place quite easily. When it's time for her supper dish, direct her to sit before placing the dish down. You should be sitting that puppy about ten thousand times a day.

Here's what will happen: Because the training happened so early, it will be indelibly entered into her mind. What you will have is a dog who automatically sits nicely when other dogs would be jumping up, pawing, and grabbing. It works. It works because by the time she is old enough to think about it, she won't. She'll just sit nicely when she doesn't know what else to do.

As a novice puppy owner, I for some reason taught my sheltie this trick. It was sit, sit, sit for everything. When he was seven months old, we played ball in the park. His ball rolled down an embankment that led directly to Highway 163. Naturally the puppy ran right after it. Completely terrified, I yelled his name. He sat. He sat very nicely, in fact. Why? Because he didn't know what he was supposed to do. In his head, When in doubt, sit. Ten years later, he's still sitting nicely when he wants something. When another dog is in trouble and getting scolded, Noël sits. If we have human visitors over for dinner and he thinks he can con one out of a tidbit, he sits. Whenever he wants to use his cuteness to hustle a human, he sits. It makes life very pleasant. It's a reflex. That's what you want, too. Whatever chaos may be going on, you can count on one thing for sure: the little sheltie

will be sitting nicely, since he learned long ago that you don't
get scolded if you sit.

Follow!

The Monks of New Skete, in *The Art of Raising a Puppy*, introduce a wonderful game. I call it the Follow Game. Take the
puppy into your fenced yard and call him to "Follow!" Use your
most animated, happy voice. Pat your leg, whistle, whatever it
takes to entice the pup into following you. Ramble around, make
some turns. While the puppy is close to you, PRAISE HIM.
"Good puppy! Good follow!" If the pup ambles off, call him
back in with a happy "Puppy, follow!"

The monks recommend ten minutes a day. The Follow
Game is wonderful because it orients the pup. He learns to pay
attention to you. He discovers that sticking close to the handler
and paying attention are very rewarding. Instill these values in
the baby now and you just might survive adolescence. Puppies
who play the Follow Game learn the command "Heel" very
easily. You can help this along by orienting the pup toward your
left side while you're playing the Follow Game. Try to get a
good game going at least once a day for thirty days. The rewards
are great.

Leash Training

Pups fight leash training. They twirl around, pull and tug, or sit
down and impersonate a mule. If leash training is not started
early enough, active resistance is inevitable. Also, puppies need
to learn to associate the leash with something pleasant and positive. That will put them in a better frame of mind to accept
restraint.

Before teaching your puppy the heel command, play some
Round Robin Recalls, also recommended by the Monks of New
Skete. Getting a puppy to come when she is called is easy. She
can't wait to get there. She doesn't like to be away from you.
In the round-robin game, everyone sits on the floor and takes
turns holding the puppy's leash and calling her. Reel her in
gently, gushing and praising up a storm as she approaches. Al-

ways go wild with praise when a dog comes when called. Be
sure all the players know they should make an enormous fuss
over the puppy when she arrives.

This game serves two purposes. First, it teaches the puppy
that coming when she is called is a smart thing to do, since that
guarantees generous amounts of praise and petting. Second, the
game helps with leash training, because the puppy has learned
to associate the leash with positive feelings. She'll be much less
afraid of the leash after a few round-robin games. Invite your
friends over to take turns calling the puppy in. If your friends
don't flock right over to play this, join a dog club. Make new
friends who have their priorities in order.

Both the Follow Game and the Round Robin Recall are also
useful with adult dogs, especially those who haven't been well
socialized to humans. They can do wonders for shy dogs.

Heel!

Now that the puppy is used to her leash, you can start teaching
the heel command. We teach it differently with puppies. None
of that jerk-and-release stuff. Cash in on the Follow Game. Give
the command "Puppy, heel!" and lure her close to your left leg
with the animated, happy voice you've been using for the Follow
Game. The puppy will think this is just a variation on that game.
Be effusive with your praise when the pup is trotting along at
your left side. She does not have to do a flawless, competition-
worthy heel at this point. The idea is to prevent her from learning to drag you down the street. Eventually, as you continue
training, you will demand near-perfection. For now, it's supposed to be fun for both of you.

All of the other basic commands can be found in the chapter
"ABCs." The techniques for teaching them are the same for
puppies as adults.

Just remember the overall agenda of the Puppy Head Start
Program: Training is fun, fun, fun! It's a wonderful game. It's
all one huge game. Get an early start. Then watch what happens
as the pup matures. You'll be the envy of all your friends. Perfecting the obedience commands will be a breeze. Obedience
will be much easier for your dog to learn because it will come

naturally. She has already learned to pay attention to you. She has learned that sticking close to her handler brings great rewards. She knows she must come when she is called. She knows, most of all, who her Alpha is. She's a secure, happy puppy. She's also a joy to live with.

MATERIAL LESSONS

If my Jet were human, she would be Madonna. Gorgeous, intelligent, brash, pushy, ambitious, materialistic, imperialistic, and at times just plain *bad*. Like her human counterpart, Jet has a marked, if incongruous, maternal streak. One fine day, during Bruno's stay at "puppy camp," the Material Dog was plopped under her favorite tree, enjoying a chewy. Bruno approached. Jet ignored him—until he crossed the invisible line defining her space. Silently, she flashed him her full set of lovely teeth. Bruno jumped back and offered up a play bow. Getting no response, he jumped sideways a few times in a vain attempt to lure Jet out of chewy heaven. Precocious little squirt Bruno again approached and again crossed the line in the sand. This time Jet added sound effects. She flashed her teeth with a snarl. Again Bruno hopped backward and did the play-bow routine. Then slow learner Bruno headed Jet's way, one more time. Again he was ignored until he violated Jet's free zone. Enough was apparently enough. Jet picked Bruno up by the scruff, gave him a good growl, and literally tossed him onto the ground, well outside the zone of foreseeable danger.

After that, Bruno respected Jet's space and her unassailable right to possess and control all things chewy. Jet's impromptu seminar impressed Bruno's owners, who were visiting. She gave a flawlessly executed demo of the hierarchy of corrections. When the milder corrections didn't get through, she escalated. Unlike dogs, owners have a tough time with corrections, especially with puppies. We worry that we'll scare them. They won't like us. (Bruno liked Jet just fine.) So we undercorrect our dogs too often. "No, no, no, NO! Don't do that! Stop that!" On and on and on it goes. We end up *nagging* our dogs. It never works. The dog thinks we're whining. We sound distraught all the time. The dog has to wonder if we are really Alpha material.

When Jet picked up Bruno and tossed him, there was nothing remotely tender about it. She had a point to make and she made it. Bruno, of course, was not injured. That was not her intent, and Bruno instinctively understood that. He was not afraid of the big dog. He did what all little squirts do: he tested limits. He wanted to see just how far he could get. He found out, most emphatically. He didn't need to do it again. He learned a lesson that is important to his survival: Don't try to take valuables away from Big Dogs. If Jet had been weak and ineffectual in teaching this early lesson, poor Bruno might have gone on to pull the same stunts on a Big Dog who was less kindly disposed toward puppies—with disastrous results.

You have to step in and take over where your dog's mother left off. It's up to you to teach the pup what he needs to know. Adult dogs understand this responsibility. In a wolf pack, all the adults help care for the puppies. It takes a pack to raise a puppy. An owner told me recently she could *never* growl at her dog the way I growled at Thunder. After all, she insisted, her dog is *little*. Aaahh. Of course. The Small Dog Exemption. To this owner, it's kinder to whip the dog into a perpetual emotional frenzy with nonstop harping, griping, and nagging. The poor dog hasn't a clue as to what the owner wants. It's all buried in the barrage. This kind of undercorrecting produces neurotic dogs. They know you're upset all the time, but they can't figure out why, or what to do about it. That's why they act out.

 MAMA REALLY DOES KNOW BEST

Make a special point of locating a mama dog with pups under four months of age. Call some breeders of a breed you especially like. Ask to make an appointment to observe litter behavior. Explain that you're a student of canine behavior. Really good breeders will help you; they support education and love to show off their pups' health and temperament. They may be fussy about hygiene, however. Do not be offended if you are met at the door with a bottle of Chlorox. Then, go watch and have fun. (If you can't find a litter of pups near you, try to find at least one under-four-months pup and adult.)

Make notes of the following:

Did the mama dog administer any discipline? What kind? With what result?

As you watch the pups, try to identify:

Which is the most dominant? Which is the most submissive? How do they demonstrate it?

CHAPTER TWO

Adolescence

Following the puppy training program requires a leap of faith. Somewhere around the forty-kabillionth "NO BITES!" you will start to question whether any of it will ever sink in. It will. Canine learning is cumulative. Even though you're not seeing results right away, the job is getting done. Try to think more globally for a few moments. Yes, the "Puppy, sit!" commands really are sinking in. But there is more going on than that. By starting your pup on the right path early you've taught her the most valuable lesson of all: you are Alpha. You're a very good Alpha. A firm, consistent, limit-setting, loving Alpha. Some puppies require more repetition than others when learning a command, but that's the small stuff. By giving the puppy commands and insisting on compliance, you are teaching her how the world works. All of the hard work and frustration you endured during Puppy Head Start was designed to get you through the next challenge: adolescence.

Throughout this book, I emphasize the differences between humans and canines. You're learning that dogs do not think the way we do. Here is the one and only exception: Canine adolescents are exactly like human adolescents.

If we took a survey, I'm pretty sure we'd find that all dogs

in all training classes in the world are around eight months old.
For weeks, your little puppy can't let you out of her sight. She
sticks to you like glue, even getting underfoot. You have no
reservations about taking her into your unfenced front yard.
She'll never run off, you insist. This blissful state lasts a few
weeks. Then, off she goes after a cat and it takes you fifteen
minutes of chasing around the neighborhood to get her back.
The same puppy who bounded up to you gleefully when you
called her name now gazes away and ambles off in the other
direction. You've got a teenager in your house.

Luckily, you followed the puppy training program. When
canine adolescence strikes, it will be in a less virulent form than
that found in uneducated dogs. You may barely notice you've
got a teenager in the house. The dog was conditioned to accept
your leadership. She trusts you. You've convinced her you know
what you're doing. Remember, dog learning is cumulative. All
of your good work has been stockpiled away in her mind. You've
earned the dog's respect and that will go a long way toward
reducing her need to test limits. Oh, she may not listen quite
as well as she used to, and may try a few experimental goofy
stunts during your training sessions, but keep working right
through it.

Cumulative dog learning can also work against you. There's
the little puppy who growled when you got too close to her food
dish. Everyone giggled. It was cute. It was cute until she got to
be six months old and bit one of the children. The puppy had
learned, all right. She had learned that pushing the humans
around is perfectly acceptable behavior.

There's also a form of passive puppy raising. The owners
don't set limits or make any attempt to train the puppy. "Oh,
he's just a puppy!" they insist. "He'll outgrow the [jumping up,
chewing, biting—fill in the blank]." These dogs show up in
school at six or eight months of age with an enormous range of
obnoxious behaviors. Again, cumulative learning was at work.
By repeatedly engaging in the same behaviors, with no negative
consequences, the puppy learned that those behaviors were just
fine. Now, of course, the behaviors have become firmly entrenched and fixing them is going to take a heck of a lot more
work. And the dog is bigger, bolder, and more independent than

he was as a baby. Here's a reality check: Next time you're on the fence about whether to correct a puppy behavior, ask yourself, Would I tolerate this behavior in a 140-pound rottweiler? If the answer is no, correct it!

Without proper puppy education, the dogs have not only failed to learn good manners, but they haven't learned their place in the pecking order. As teenagers, they aren't particularly invested in recognizing you as the all-powerful Alpha figure in their lives.

In other words, *many behavior problems develop in puppyhood, but do not show up until adolescence.*

An owner liked roughhousing and playing "Sic 'em" games with his rottie-mix puppy. They wrestled and played on the floor with great abandon and lots of puppy play bites. They played lots of tug of war. The owner would give the "Sic 'em" command and the pup would chase his friends around the house barking and snapping. At seven months of age, the owner attempted to move the large pup off his bed. The pup growled. Two weeks later, the owner suffered a bad bite while picking up the dog's food dish. The puppy had learned that biting humans was acceptable. His natural prey drive was pushed into high gear by the "Sic 'em" games and he learned that humans are appropriate prey. He had come to regard his owner as a littermate and social equal. The dog started taking the games more seriously as his hormone levels increased. He's now a full-fledged, card-carrying terrorist.

REFORM SCHOOL

Okay, maybe you didn't have this book and now you have an obnoxious teenage canine in your pack. What's a good owner to do? Phase one is to review the puppy sections and start over. Get a crate. Put some structure into Fido's world. If you're having mild limit-testing behavior problems, a return to puppyhood and basic obedience training will get you on the right track. By mild limit-testing, I mean the dog still jumps on people to say hello and doesn't come when she is called. She needs to learn to respect your authority and to show some proper manners.

Growling, biting, destroying property, and generally being

out of control are more serious problems and require more serious work to correct.

GOING HORMONAL

Much obnoxious teenage behavior is hormone-driven. Get the dog fixed. The sooner, the better. Don't wait until the behaviors become entrenched. Owners often say they want to breed the dog because they like her so much. They say they want a puppy "just like her." It's understandable. It's sort of an emotional annuity against the day they lose their pet.

The problem is, without a thorough understanding of the science of genetics and an intimate knowledge of both parents' ancestry, it's unlikely that the puppies will be anything like either parent. The entire litter could be a throwback to several generations past. It's anyone's guess what kind of health and temperament problems will crop up. And then there's the big question: What will you do with all those puppies? Sure, all your friends say they love your dog, too. They all insist they want a puppy from her. Watch them evaporate right around the seven-week mark.

Owners often think their dogs are breedable because they are AKC registered. Well, my car is DMV registered, but it's still a junkbox. Registration means I can prove it's a Mazda, not a Chevy. That's all it proves. It's the same with AKC registration. You can prove your chow chow really is a chow chow. That's all. And fraudulent papers are a big problem as well.

Week after week, students appear in my classes with problem dogs. Dogs that try to murder every dog they see. Or every human. Hyper dogs. Nervous, high-strung dogs. Dogs who bunny-hop when they run (making me suspect hip dysplasia). Dogs with missing teeth. Dogs the owners are completely unable to control. When we talk about spaying and neutering, most of the owners insist: "But I want to *breed* her [or him]!" Why? In what way will the breed be improved? Luckily, many of the students eventually see the light and get the dogs fixed. We give them lots of praise for this. Goooood Owner!

CHAPTER THREE

Developing the Dog/Owner Bond: Communication

The dog/owner relationship is the foundation for a well-adjusted, polite dog. When a dog has behavior problems, they usually can be traced back to something going haywire between the dog and the owner. If your dog isn't listening attentively to you and following directions, she is failing to recognize you as the Alpha in her life.

COMMUNICATION

A well-educated dog is a lot less apt to get into trouble than an ill-educated one. Soon you'll be working on teaching basic commands. That will help to create the right kind of dog/owner bond. With many dogs, behavior problems start to drop off as they become more educated.

Does your dog do as he pleases? Hang out on the furniture? Ignore commands? Destroy your belongings? You just may have an Alpha Wanna-be on your hands. If so, the dog's behavior is entirely correct—*for an Alpha.* The problem is, Alpha dogs are no fun to live with. Actually, it's a dog's confusion about who the Alpha really is that sets up a lot of problems. As clever as your dog may be, he cannot be allowed to be the Alpha. We have made the world an unsafe place for dogs. Dogs cannot roam free anymore. They get hit by cars if they run loose. Humans have created these hazards, and therefore we have the responsibility to behave like proper Alphas. Your dog can't simply go out and get his own dinner (he has no credit cards). You have to take over.

THE SECRET AGENDA: WE'RE NOT TRAINING DOGS, WE'RE TRAINING HUMANS TO BE WOLVES

Well, sort of. Your dog's brain is not constructed in such a way that he can communicate with words. What this means is that you will have to make the effort to learn your dog's language, not the other way around. The good news is that dogs are adaptable, hardy creatures and they hardly ever laugh at us when we make mistakes.

Obedience training is a step in the right direction. But there is more to it than sit, stay, and heel. Your goal is to develop the best possible relationship with your dog. Good communication will help get you there.

Remember, every wolf- or dog pack has an Alpha. The Alpha directs and organizes hunting activity and keeps unruly wolves in line. The Alpha reigns supreme. Dogs, just like wolves, are obsessed with this hierarchy business. Two dogs cannot meet without doing some degree of rank-order sorting. (They do it so well, we don't always notice.) Only the best, strongest and most powerful pack member gets to be the Alpha.

Do wolves resent their dictator? Do they sit around in closed den meetings, plotting an overthrow? No! That's human behavior. Canine subordinates adore their Alpha. When you watch a documentary about wolves, look for the greeting ritual subordinates bestow upon their Alpha. There's lots of twirling, dancing, and wolf kissing. They all feel better when the Alpha is around. They feel more secure. Try to keep in mind that dogs, like their wolf ancestors, are genetically programmed to follow a strong Alpha. They *need* a hierarchy. Until you have firmly established one, behavior problems won't get better and your dog won't be as happy as he could be.

If your dog considers himself the Alpha, it's only because nobody told him he wasn't. Dogs, programmed to lead or be led, feel extreme tension in the absence of a strong Alpha. Your dog is worried because his instincts are telling him he is not safe and he had better do something, quick. He wants to feel better about his lot in life, so he does the only thing he can do: he becomes the Alpha. That is always bad news. Your dog isn't capable of being the pack leader in our world. Deep down, your dog knows it, too.

Alpha dogs don't do as they're told, unless they happen to feel like it. Alphas growl when you try to take their bones away; Alphas chew anything that strikes them as chewable; Alphas pick fights; Alphas don't necessarily come when they are called. In other words, Alphas do as they please. Don't blame the dog! His behavior is perfectly correct for an Alpha. Alpha dogs also feel justified in demanding attention or petting. Inside, your dog senses he's not really cut out for the CEO position.

 THE ALPHA WANNA-BE CHECKLIST

Does your dog:

- *Ever* growl at *any* human?
- Hang out on the furniture?
- Refuse to get off your bed?
- Push past you going out the door?
- Demand attention, treats, or games by pawing at you?

If the answer to any of the above questions is yes, you may have an Alpha Wanna-be. Make a list of some other bossy, pushy, demanding Alpha behaviors you have observed in your dog.

The good news is that a dog who is simply dominant has excellent rehab potential. *Your* task is to become more dominant; once the dog is sufficiently impressed with your leadership skills, he'll happily abdicate the throne.

The bad news is that, left unchecked, Alpha Wanna-bes almost invariably develop aggression problems. Enforcing their will with their teeth is completely logical to a dominant dog. These guys were the bullies of their litters and they're treating you as if you were a littermate.

But remember, he honestly feels that he must take over, or he won't survive. He's just not good at it.

THE COUP

It should be easy to understand why your leader of the pack must be ousted. The question is, How? He won't be impressed if you hold an election. Remember, a wolf pack is not a democracy. There's only one way to overthrow a canine tyrant: You must become the Alpha. In wolfdom, such overthrows can be gory affairs. Fortunately, you have an advantage: your intelligence. Accept this: You are going to have to learn to be an Alpha wolf. That includes learning the language, customs, and cultural nuances.

WOLFESE

Yes, you do have to learn a new language. Fortunately, it's not a difficult one. If you have a flair for dramatic acting, you'll be a natural. Wolves in a pack are a silent species. Yet they stay in constant communication with one another. This is essential to survival because if one wolf alerts on the scent of prey, he must notify the rest of the pack quickly. To facilitate this exchange of information, wolves in a pack monitor each other all the time. How do they communicate? *Body language.* All dogs and wolves are Ph.D.-level body language experts. Observe two dogs living in the same household; notice how much they watch each other. A thorough sniffing may be required after they have been separated for only a few minutes.

Dogs communicate all the time, without words. The way a dog holds his tail, for example, sends a signal about how he's feeling. Another dog can read this accurately. Dogs never misunderstand each other. They don't have language to clutter things up. A good handler can prevent a dog fight before so much as a growl has been uttered. Perhaps she saw one dog give the other the "hard eye." It's the canine equivalent of two rivals throwing gang signs at each other on a street corner. A good handler will correct that hard eye sternly and praise the dog for glancing away and going about his business. You can be that fluent in Wolfese, too.

The best part is, you have a tutor available twenty-four hours a day. Spend some time just watching your dog. Get familiar with how she holds her ears and tail when she's happy or excited. Note the expressiveness of her face.

When you are walking your dog and encounter another dog, observe the Sniffing Ceremony. One dog will sniff the other, while the sniffee holds completely still. Then the sniffer reciprocates and allows himself to be sniffed. This ritual is a common throwback to wolf behavior. Would you believe that by the time the ceremony is under way, the dogs have already worked out a dominance hierarchy? That's how good they are at this. The dog who agreed to be the sniffee first has allowed the other dog to assert dominance. *Never yank your dog away during the ceremony.* The other dog will resent this social faux paw and can be offended enough to attack. That's how important all of this posturing and ritual business is to the dog. Fortunately, your dog knows what to do.

If you encounter a friendly dog, watch for the Play Bow Ritual. One dog will drop his front end to the ground, rear end high in the air, tail wagging at warp speed. If this doesn't get the desired response (a game), the fun-seeker may jump sideways a few times, to invite a chase. If a strange dog approaches and goes into a play bow, relax. His intentions could not be more honorable.

The owners of a wonderful golden retriever were concerned about what they perceived as aggression toward their toddler. The dog kept hip-bumping the child. Some dogs use the hip-bump technique instead of the Play Bow Ritual to induce games. The dog was trying to get the baby to play with him.

See, this language isn't as foreign as you thought. You have already observed your canine friend communicating in Wolfese many times. You just didn't know the language.

 COMMUNICATION: BODY LANGUAGE

Spend some time each day just observing your dog. Pay close attention to his ears and tail. You'll notice these parts are very active.

In your Dog Log, make some notes about what the dog is doing, and what the dog's body language looks like. If you like to draw, feel free. Don't forget to make some notes about what is going on at the time. Keep an eye on the dog's facial expression also, especially the mouth.

Example: Spot and I were out for a walk. We met a lady walking a little puppy. Spot sniffed the puppy while the puppy held perfectly still. Then the puppy jumped sideways a few times. Spot's ears were back and his tail was wagging. He was panting, too.

Spot's body language was completely normal. The puppy stood still and allowed the sniffing, thus signaling respect for Spot's higher rank. The position of Spot's ears was his way of looking smaller and less intimidating to the puppy. Spot's panting was the canine equivalent of a friendly laugh, especially if you could actually *hear* the pant. The little fun seeker's sideways jumps were an attempt to initiate a game. Adult dogs are normally friendly with young puppies. If Spot's tail was held at about mid height and it was a fast side-to-side wag, he was using his tail to say hello in a friendly manner.

After a week or so of recording your observations, you will find yourself reading your dog quite efficiently. This information will help you when you start teaching obedience. Is your dog enjoying his lessons? Should you be praising more effusively? How about your corrections? Are you getting clear signals of respect?

What does your dog look like when meeting new people? Is he happy and confident or does he need more socialization?

Knowing how your dog is feeling is an important component of establishing communication. His body language will tell you loud and clear.

 HIERARCHY OBSERVATIONS

Next time you and your dog encounter another dog while you're out on a walk, observe:

- What did the dogs do?
- How did they use their ears and tails?
- Were there any vocalizations? If so, what kind?
- Who held still to be sniffed first?
- Then what happened?
- How long did the Sniffing Ceremony last?
- What were the dogs' relative rankings?

You've just learned a *lot* about your dog. Was she willing to be the submissive one and be first sniffee? How did she handle herself in the presence of a strange dog? Did she immediately drop into a play bow? If so, she is probably a young dog, well socialized to other dogs. To her, playing is more important than social status. Or did the dogs circle around each other for a while before the actual ceremony got under way? If so, they both consider themselves fairly high-ranking. Which one finally agreed to submit?

Use every opportunity to observe your dog's interaction with other dogs, especially in the all-important Sniffing Ceremony. You'll be learning how she feels about herself.

LITTLE THINGS THAT MEAN A LOT

To be truly fluent in your dog's language, you will have to learn to use the nonverbal communication that canids use with each other. Small gestures can have powerful meanings to a dog. Eye contact is a good example: an Alpha has an absolute right to demand eye contact from a subordinate, or to refuse eye contact, at Alpha's whim. An Alpha is never the first to look away; that's a gesture of submission. Never look a strange dog directly in the eye, he may take it as a challenge.

Dogs often act as if they will fight to the death over who gets to go out the door first. From now on, *you* go out the door first. If you continue to let Fido plow ahead of you out the door, you're giving up a lot of dog status points.

You've heard the old bromide about letting sleeping dogs lie. Well, it's wrong. Don't tiptoe around a sleeping dog. You, as Alpha, have a right to go where you please, and your subordinate must accommodate you. This is especially important if your dog is on the dominant side, which many problem dogs are. If you want to get past Rover while he's snoozing, order him to "MOVE!" in your most authoritative Alpha voice. If he doesn't move, push him out of your way. Praise him once he's out of your path. The same applies when your dog is standing or sitting in your way. With dominant problem dogs, wake them up and move them now and then, just to demonstrate that you can.

These gestures may seem trivial to you, but they are not minor matters to your dog. All of these little gestures add up, and you'll be helping your dog learn to show you proper respect.

BARK BARK

Your dog also has a unique language of barks. Some dogs have an entire repertoire of woofs and warbles all their own. You needn't learn to bark to communicate with your dog, but understanding your dog does require some attention to her special language.

Dogs have more than one bark. When you come home, does your dog greet you with a high-pitched yappy bark? She's telling you she is excited and happy to see you. Many dogs have a high-pitched play bark; you'll hear it when she wants her ball to be tossed.

Have you heard your dog's low-pitched, gutteral bark? Sometimes it sounds like a combination of a bark and growl. That's your dog's warning bark. It means "Back off!" It's the territorial bark and it's meant to be threatening.

Is it true that a barking dog won't bite? No! There is always an anxiety component in a bark. Something has stimulated the dog and he's discharging some anxiety. A dog preparing for a dominance assault may not utter a single bark. He's feeling confident and in command of the situation. A fearful dog, on the other paw, may bark up a storm. When strangers approach my house, my Jet and Cassius both bark, but Jet adds a menacing snarl to all who get too close to her fence. Cash just woofs and woofs. Which one is more likely to bite? Unequivocally, Jet takes that honor, and a snarl from her is a serious threat. Cash barks at people because he's excited; he's gleefully announcing the arrival of new playmates. The last thing Cassius wants is for people to go away. How many different barks does your dog have?

 BARKING

No, You don't have to bark. In your Dog Log, list the number of different barks you hear from your dog. Try to figure out what they mean.

Example: When I came home from work today, Spot jumped, twirled, and barked his high-pitched yappy bark. He was excited and happy.

How many different barks does your dog have? What is he trying to tell you?

Again, your goal is to understand what your dog is feeling by learning his special language. Aggression problems are often misdiagnosed because owners simply fail to interpret barks. There's a big difference between a confident dog issuing an appropriate warning to a suspicious-looking stranger and a fearful dog in a complete panic. Listen carefully! A rat-tat-tat "machine gun" bark is an anxiety signal. What's happening? Is the dog isolated too much? Or, if the dog is responding to a clearly non-threatening situation, is he a prospective fear-biter?

TAIL TALES

How many times have you been told, "Oh, don't worry, he won't bite. His tail is wagging." It's a testimony to the good nature of the dog that only about five million people are bitten each year. *Dogs do attack with their tails wagging.* Like a bark, a tail wag can have more than one meaning. Anxiety is an element in tail behavior, too. A dog feeling dominant and in control of the situation holds his tail high and still. A fast side to side wag is usually a friendly, happy wag. Tail up high, with a slow side to side wag is a serious dominance signal; the dog is ready to challenge any and all disbelievers. Fearful dogs can really confuse you: the tail may be wagging furiously as the dog prepares to attack. The fearful dog is anxious and ambivalent; he's unpredictable.

Ears and tails tell you a lot about what's going on with your dog. Dogs with stand-up ears, like German shepherds, are easier to read. Ears up or forward signals alertness and confidence. Ears pinned back is a submissive position. Again, fearful dogs will confuse you. Ears back and head low can be a friendly, submissive signal. Or the dog may be feeling fearful enough to strike.

A dog's mouth will give you some reliable information. Are

the lips pulled back? He's revving up. Showing teeth is not good news. Much of this canine body language is stereotypical, but each dog has his own special code. Observing your dog carefully will help you learn to read your friend.

NATURE VERSUS NURTURE

You'll hear a lot of talk among dog people about *temperament*. Just what do we mean when we talk about your dog's temperament? We're talking about basic *traits* the dog has that remain stable over time. They're pretty much what the dog was born with. When we talk about purebred dogs, you'll hear that a given dog has "correct" temperament. Each recognized breed has a standard, which includes certain elements of temperament. For example, if you tell me you own a Border collie who has high energy levels and is extremely intelligent, we can say your dog has correct temperament for her breed. Your Border collie is not ever going to be a sluggish, laid-back kind of dog.

Does that mean that if your dog has traits you aren't happy with, you're stuck? Not at all. Thanks to their wolf ancestors, dogs are amazingly adaptable. Your Border collie will always be a high-energy dog. That does not mean she cannot learn to control her energy. She certainly can. She can learn to hold a nice long down-stay in the house. As a member of a fine working breed, she'll thoroughly enjoy being trained.

Your dog also has a personality. That's the effect of the dog's environment, especially her interactions with humans and other animals. Puppies who are raised in a rich, stimulating environment and are exposed to a variety of experiences develop into poised, confident, outgoing dogs.

In human psychology, the debate has gone on for decades about the influence of environment versus heredity. Fortunately, because of dogs' great capacity to adapt to their environment, very little about them is set in concrete. While it's certainly preferable to start with a dog with excellent temperament, it's not essential. A dog can learn. It is useful, however, to learn about your particular breed. If you have a mixed-breed dog, you'll probably notice that one or two breeds seem to dominate. Ask your vet or trainer what breeds she sees in your dog. The more you understand your dog's heritage, the easier it will be for you to anticipate which tasks will be easier to teach.

THE "C" WORD

"If *you* can't do something with him, he's going back to the pound!"

I hate these calls. Sometimes, the owner is at his wits' end and just needs to vent. That's okay. It happens. Other times, he really means it. One client actually threatened to dump the dog at the pound if *I* wouldn't take her. This after only two lessons with a badly socialized pooch who was just scared of everything.

One essential ingredient in educating your dog is *commitment*. If that's not there, if the owner is going to "wait and see how it goes," it may fail miserably. Does the owner think the dog doesn't know her owner is on the fence? Of course she does. She reads it loud and clear. It *hurts*. It confuses. Dogs don't operate this way. They don't sit around wondering how they could swap owners. Once you've had the dog for even a few days, in her heart and mind she is *yours*.

When I adopted Cassius, as baffling as it was to everyone around me, I never considered not keeping him. Sure, he was frustrating, and he got into a lot of trouble and scared the daylights out of people. Oh, well. We'll just have to work on that. Cash, of course, knew how I felt. He was a loving, affectionate dog. He desperately needed a home. Part of the reason he shaped up so nicely is because he knew he had found one.

Do you wish you had gotten another dog? One who was better behaved? One who was at least housebroken dependably? But if you had gotten this Dream Doggie, would you really be motivated to work this hard? Would you be studying diligently, trying to understand the canine mind? Probably not. But then you would have missed something precious. Because your dog's behavior was sufficiently obnoxious, you were motivated to take serious action, in the form of training and studying. When the dog shapes up (and he will), your relationship will be more than you ever imagined it could be. You'll see.

So before you start serious work with your problem pup, do

some soul-searching. Are you really committed to keeping this dog? If you are, the best is yet to come.

REAL LOVE

Not everyone should have a dog. In fact, lots of people who have them shouldn't. Caring for a dog takes time, patience, and lots of love. Of course, we all love our dogs. Don't we?

Is it real love? Or a sentimental attachment? There is a difference. Lots of owners think they love their dogs. But it looks more like sentiment—sometimes, cheap sentiment. The owner who would never make her dog do things he doesn't want to do is a sentimental owner.

Similarly, owners who don't have the "heart" to get their dog neutered are sentimental owners. And owners who want to breed their dog because they "love her so much" are being sentimental. They're not stopping to consider the ill effects on the dog, the potential for injury and complications. Spaying dramatically reduces a female dog's risk of contracting breast cancer. The breast cancer risk for females spayed prior to their first heat is virtually zero percent. The risk increases with each subsequent estrus and can be as high as 300 percent. Unspayed females are also vulnerable to uterine and ovarian cancers and the often deadly uterine infection pyometra. In cases of pyometra the uterus fills with pus and the dog becomes gravely ill. Antibiotics are often ineffective and spaying is the only sure cure. But operating on a dog when she is so ill is dangerous. This disease has been found to be directly related to hormones and is prevented completely by spaying. Male dogs enjoy lots of health benefits from neutering as well. That's in addition to the positive behavioral changes. Neutered males don't suffer from prostate disease and cancer. They don't develop testicular cancer. And they do a lot less brawling with other dogs. Real love is most definitely about spaying and neutering. It's proof not only of your real love for your own dog, but your love for dogs. Real dog lovers are appalled at the pet overpopulation problem and get their dogs fixed.

Real love also requires a good measure of veterinary intervention. True love means getting the dog to the vet when it's necessary. And then listening to what the doctor says. Even when you don't want to hear it.

Owners who feed their dog table scraps are driven by sentiment and selfishness. It makes them *feel* like loving owners. These "loving" owners kill their dogs. To prove they "love" their dogs, they give them toxic substances, like chocolate. They do it so the dogs will "love" *them.*

The owner of an obese dog insists on adding treats to her dog food. He whips up concoctions of bacon grease and other delicacies. He throws dog cookies into her dish with her food. He claims he wants to make her food "more palatable." Why? She's eating just fine. He thinks dog food must taste awful. It makes him feel good to give her treats. That's sentiment. Real love means sticking faithfully to the vet's instructions about diet and exercise.

When I consult with owners about dog behavior problems, almost invariably I find out that the dog is being given too many treats. There is certainly nothing wrong with giving your dog a little biscuit now and then, but some owners are handing out ten cookies a day. What's happening is, the owner is humanizing the dog. It's easy to do. Dogs are so much like us emotionally, it's often hard to remember that they are a different species. Nowhere is this more apparent than in the way we look at food. We humans are food-oriented. Our celebrations and holidays center around food. Who among us can honestly say he or she has never grabbed a carton of ice cream after a bad day? We associate food with love and comfort. When a toddler falls down, Mom offers a cookie and a hug. So we quite naturally and with the best of intentions offer treats to our dogs. It makes us feel more loving. But our domestic wolves don't see the whole food issue the way we do. Your dog's mother never withheld food when he misbehaved. Nor did she offer food when he was hurt or upset. No. Mama dogs feed their babies when they need to be fed. This is another important difference between humans and canines that must be understood if you are to have a healthy relationship with your dog: *Your dog does not associate food with love.*

But dogs are total opportunists, and once they learn that gazing up at you with goo-goo eyes wins them a cookie, they'll play the role for you. But they never connect this exchange with an emotional attachment. Loving owners feed their dogs a premium-quality dry feed appropriate to the dog's age and activity level and feel very good about themselves. The premium dog food companies spend about a kabillion dollars a year on research. We have excellent food available for our dogs. Extra tidbits can throw off the perfect nutritional balance. Check with your vet, breeder, and trainer about the right diet for your dog. If your dog is eating her food, if her coat is shiny and her eyes are clear and bright, leave well enough alone! Dogs, because they are dogs and not humans, do not get bored eating the same food every day. Changing food can cause gastrointestinal upset, so don't change unless you must or the vet tells you to.

Food behavior, however, does serve as another arena in which you can collect status points. Under the rules of the Pack Code, the Alpha male and female always get to dine first. Subordinates must wait and accept whatever is left over. If you've been feeding the dog her supper before you eat yours, she's getting the idea that she outranks the humans.

So what *does* love mean, from a dog's point of view? Number one on their list is *time*. Your time is the most precious commodity you have to offer your dog. Your dog loves attention, especially the focused kind she gets when you give her an obedience lesson. She really appreciates the opportunity to earn your praise. Your dog also adores your leadership skills. She feels happy and secure knowing she has a strong Alpha wolf in her pack.

Sentiment is a selfish motive. I've seen old, very sick dogs, in constant pain, too debilitated to leave their beds to eliminate. There's the poor, suffering dog, lying in her own urine. The owners won't have the dog humanely euthanized. Why? Because they "love" her too much. Actually, they're incredibly selfish. They're trying to avoid the inevitable horrible grieving process—at the dog's expense. A loving owner listens to the vet's advice, even when it hurts.

Sentimental love is all about making ourselves feel better. "Oh, I could never growl like that at my little Fluffy! I might scare her!" So little Fluffy runs around, doing whatever she pleases. Until the day she goes too far and finds herself at the pound.

Then there's Taz, the delightful boxer who does world-class down-stays. I had Taz's owner place him on a long down-stay. Then I picked up his favorite ball and bounced it around. One student was upset: "That seems terribly *cruel!*" she insisted. Taz's owner set the record straight. He explained that if Taz is going to break his down-stay for some temptation, he'd rather Taz did it while he was safely on leash than on the day his leash breaks or something else unexpected happens. *That's* a truly loving owner. He could handle Taz's few moments of frustration. He could handle it because he knows *it's in the best interest of the dog.* The only way to ensure that Taz will not someday break his stay and run out into traffic after a toy is to practice, practice, practice, with plenty of real-life-style distractions. Taz's owner loves him enough to set firm limits, when necessary. Taz will live a long and happy life because of his owner's willingness to be unsentimental.

The owner who lives with and makes excuses for a dog who snarls, growls, or actually bites is a sentimental owner. "Oh, Flopsie was upset, I shouldn't have tried to get by her while she was sleeping. . . ." This kind of sentiment can be lethal. A loving owner recognizes that there is a problem and takes action. She consults a trainer. She gets Flopsie to the vet for a checkup because she knows aggression can have medical causes. She works with the dog and with the trainer.

Then there is the sentimental owner who never puts a leash on his dog. He wants the dog to feel "free." He likes the ego gratification. He maintains his delusion that he has complete control over his dog. He doesn't seem to make the connection when his dogs keep getting hit by cars.

Sentimental love is cheap. It's not very mature. The sentimental owner is stuck at the child stage. He sees the dog as an object, not unlike a stuffed toy. The dog's needs, even the dog's *dogness,* are not considered. Lots of owners adopt dogs thinking the dog will just quietly and contentedly lie around the house all day. They have visions of a pretty dog stretched out in front of the fireplace. There's no room in there for reality. You can indeed have a dog who is contented and well-mannered in the house. But it takes work. The dog must be educated. He must learn manners. He must get sufficient exercise and quality feed.

He must get enough play. He must be kept in the best of health. He must have a job to do and a loving Alpha.

Or there is the owner who keeps the dog stuck out in the yard all day. The owner spends maybe ten minutes a day with the dog, at best. These owners actually tell me they "love" their dogs. How is that possible? Forcing the most sociable animal to live a lonely life? That's loving? Sometimes they tell me the dog is "happy." Actually, the dog has given up. He no longer bothers to misbehave or bark all night for attention. He has quit. He's just existing.

A friend commented recently that my dogs are "interesting." They're all characters. They're fun to have around. It's because they have so much human interaction: it makes for a more interesting companion. They have jobs. They engage with people. My friend is right. They are interesting. They're not bored very often. They're not little robots, however. They misbehave sometimes. But, on the whole, they're pretty wonderful. So are many of my students' dogs. Their owners care enough to educate them. The dogs do become more interesting and more fun.

When in doubt, you can always stop and ask yourself: Am I acting in the *dog's* best interest? If the answer is yes, you are indeed a truly loving owner.

 TRANSLATION, PLEASE

How might a dog interpret the following owner behavior?

I had to work late, then I hit traffic and when I *finally* got home and started dinner, I realized I had forgotten to stop and pick up dog food. So I ran to the pet supply store, raced back home, and fed Fluffy. Then we all sat down to dinner.

a. Fluffy thought, Wow, my owner must be a really good hunter, she was only gone a few minutes and came back with lots of food!

b. My owner is acting awfully stressed lately, I wonder what I did wrong.

c. Yipeee! I really am the Alpha wolf in this pack. Those subordinate humans of mine made sure I got fed first. Then I let them eat human food.

Answer: All three possible interpretations make good dogsense, but "c" requires the least abstract thinking by the dog and is probably the most logical interpretation of the owner's behavior. If you're a dog.

Can you think of some behaviors your dog has observed that he might be putting his own spin on?

 ## COMMITMENT

Make a list of everything your dog does that makes you crazy. Don't hold back! He's not going to read this.

Now, think about the day you got your dog. What made you choose him or her? Write a short paragraph about that. What do you like about your dog?

Go back over your list of crazy-making stuff. Is there anything on there that could be changed? Okay, maybe with a lot of work, but could it be changed? For example, "Dog doesn't do as he's told" is more a statement about handler error than about the dog. Perhaps the dog doesn't understand what he's being told to do. Or no one has made it clear to the dog that humans outrank him and therefore are entitled to issue commands. This is an entirely fixable problem.

On the other paw, if "Dog sheds" is an important item on your list, we may have a problem. Could a groomer be of help? How about a change of diet?

Often, when someone in the household is unhappy with the dog over *nonfixable* problems, e.g., "Dog is too big," there is something else going on. Commitment probably is not there. And, rest assured, the dog's size is not the real issue. Something else is. It's the Alpha's job to get to the bottom of these kinds of conflicts.

REAL LOVE

List three things you have done that were not in your dog's best interest, though you thought you were acting out of love.

Example: We didn't have the heart to get Fang neutered. Early this morning, he crashed through the plateglass window in our living room while our neighbor was walking his female, who is in heat. Fang is still in surgery. The vet doesn't know if he'll make it, he's lost so much blood.

 OTHER OWNERS

Spend the next week paying special attention to the other owners you observe. Can you identify any cheap sentiment where the Real Love should be? Make a list. For example:

- My neighbor told me she quit taking her dog to obedience class because it was too much hassle.
- My other neighbors refuse to allow their dog in the house, even at night, because she sheds.
- I caught a lady in the park feeding her dog chocolate candy.

During your observation week, also be on the lookout for good dog owners.

Example: My sister made a vet appointment for her dog for tomorrow morning, just because she thought the dog didn't look quite right. She claims the dog looks "droopy," so she's bringing her in for a checkup.

My brother, who has an expensive purebred dog, took him in to be neutered.

WHAT I DID FOR LOVE

List three ways you can show your dog Real Love, right now. For example:

- Give him an obedience lesson.
- Make an appointment at the vet for a checkup and teeth cleaning.
- Supervise the kids to make sure they don't slip the dog any of their snacks.
- Give him a big hug. Right now!

 BY INVITATION ONLY

How does your dog let you know she wants to play? Does she drop the ball in your lap? Offer up a play bow? Or a high-pitched yap? Some sideways jumps?

Does she have a hierarchy of play invites? For example, there's the young Lab who drops the ball in her owner's lap. If that doesn't work, she'll sit down and start barking.

How pushy is your dog when inviting you to play? Is she polite about it or do you feel bullied?

Keep track of how your dog extends invitations. If she's really pushy about it, consider her an Alpha Wanna-be.

How often does your dog invite you to play? What time(s) of day? A happy, well-adjusted dog wants to play often. Some dogs just need to learn to ask more politely.

Understanding your dog's normal moods and play patterns not only can help you get to know your dog better, but will make you more alert for changes that could signal that the dog isn't feeling well. Really knowing and observing your dog is good for you and for your dog's health. You'll get the dog to the vet much more promptly if you recognize when your dog is less playful and active than usual.

CHAPTER FOUR

Behavior Problems

She's Trying, but She Doesn't Get It

The majority of our dogs fall into this category. They really want to please, but can't figure out what we want. Often, they can't figure out who we are. Are we fellow pack members? Littermates? Or are we Alphas?

"Fluffy, sit. No, sit, I know you know how to do this, now c'mon Fluff, I said sit! Sit, sit, sit, oh, that's it, Fluffy, good girl, I knew you could do it, do you want a treat? . . ."

Poor Fluffy. What's a dog to do? She's earnestly struggling to figure out what her owner is saying. She may actually even sit, taking a wild guess at what her owner wants.

Alphas maintain order using a lot of posturing and displays. They know how to command attention. They get pretty theatrical about it, if necessary. Dogs love drama. They use their voices, their body language, and eye contact to rule the pack. That's what Fluffy is looking for. To her ears, her owner's barrage sounds like *whining*. Her littermates whined. She was allowed to ignore them; they were social equals. So Fluffy is perfectly justified in tuning out her owner.

Fluffy's owner has fallen into the common trap of talking to the dog as if she were human. She doesn't feel comfortable delivering a forceful "Fluffy, SIT!" It seems rather *rude*. If you addressed a human coworker this way, it would come across as obnoxious. Fluffy, however, is a dog. She can recognize a "command voice." When Fluffy sits, she has earned your best "praise voice." This also does not come naturally for us. Try "Goooood Giiiirrrrl, Fluffy! What a good girl!" in your most animated, excited voice. You can gauge the effectiveness of your praise voice. Does Fluffy bounce up to you, tail high, beaming and glowing? If so, you've got the hang of it. This is one of the many reasons a good obedience school is so important. You'll feel less ridiculous if everyone else is gushing right along with you.

We women especially have to work on voice control. Often, owners report that the dog responds only to their husbands or other adult males. Male voices tend to be more authoritative. Ours are higher pitched and less commanding. But we're much better praisers. Men have a tough time getting the right amount of gooiness in their voices.

At the same time, all owners must learn to correct their dogs properly. For that, we really have to go to the wolves. An Alpha scolds a misbehaving pack member with stern growls and glares. The sound effects are quite impressive. The subordinate knows he's really not about to be murdered, but offers up a show of submission anyway. The subordinate wolf's ears go back and his head lowers as he tries to look smaller. What he's saying is, "Okay, I'm sorry I displeased you! You outrank me."

Giving a good correction is no easy skill for a human to learn. There are excellent instructors available to you, fortunately. Adult dogs. Try to observe an adult with a young puppy. It doesn't have to be his or her own puppy. Any adult dog will discipline an unruly pup. It's another wolf thing. All adult wolves are expected to help care for young wolf pups. They act as babysitters when Mama Wolf needs an outing.

Interestingly, adult dogs will tolerate a great deal of nonsense from puppies. Puppies freely gnaw ears and tails of their social superiors with no repercussions. Adults will, however, set limits when they see fit. Unless the adult is severely psychologically disturbed, it's pretty safe to put adults and puppies together. (*Note*: An adult dog who tries to actually harm a young puppy is, by definition, severely psychologically disturbed. Dogs have strong inhibitions against harming puppies, a trait essential for the survival of any species.)

Watch an adult with a puppy under four months of age. Observe what happens when the precocious little one makes a move for the big dog's toy or chewy. You'll likely hear a good staccato growl/snarl. You may even see some teeth. You'll note the adult dog does not attempt to reason with the puppy; there is no negotiating. It's "KNOCK IT OFF!" in no uncertain terms. Some more dominant puppies will back off and try again, upping the ante. If the youngster doesn't get the picture soon, you may shortly see him scooting into the nearest corner with his tail between his legs and his ears pasted to his head. He's not harmed in the least, apart from the social mortification of it all. The adult may snarl, snap, even roll the puppy over and pin him. All of these rituals signal clearly to the puppy: "I am your social superior. You will respect me."

Now, watch what happens next. Thinking in human terms, as we are prone to do, wouldn't we expect the puppy to be pretty upset with the adult? After all, the poor pup got snarled and growled at—pretty rude behavior, no? We certainly would not appreciate being treated that way by our human companions. But what will happen, once the puppy regains his composure, is that he'll start tagging along with the adult. Usually, sort of a hero worship thing develops. The puppy will actually seem to like the adult better after such an incident.

Here's what happened, from the puppy's perspective: The adult established her dominance. She behaved like an Alpha. All dogs instinctively look for and want to please the Alpha. The puppy feels better. He's more secure now that there is a strong Alpha figure on the scene to keep him safe. His genes tell him that his best chance for survival is to stay close to the Alpha. It's simply the natural order of things. The adult has earned the puppy's *respect*. This is the most important concept in dogdom. Above all else, *respect*. Dogs love the one they respect the most.

Like wolves, dogs also love other subordinate pack members and bond to them. But it is not the same quality of deep love, trust, and admiration a dog feels for the Alpha. That is your goal. You want your dog to obey because it is the dog's greatest pleasure in life to please the beloved Alpha. You do not want your dog to obey because she is afraid of you, or intimidated by you. An Alpha commands by earning respect, not by terrorizing the subordinates. It's an art.

Thus, learning to correct your dog properly is essential. It's not easy, but you can do it. You must model your corrections after the Alpha wolf's. Or, if you prefer, think of a mama dog with her litter. They are a replica of an Alpha wolf with the pack.

DOGS WHO UNDERSTAND,
BUT DISOBEY ANYWAY

First, be certain the dog really does understand. For example, there is the treat-trained dog who sits nicely on command when you have a biscuit in your hand, but ignores commands when you are treat-free. We see this a lot. Step one is to wean the dog off the training treats by giving them only sometimes, and eventually eliminating them entirely. As you're working on becoming an Alpha, the dog's devotion to you alone will be enough to elicit the sit.

Or the dog who follows commands in class but runs wild at home. The dog hasn't learned yet that you are Alpha, and your commands must be followed anytime, anywhere. Start working the dog in a variety of locations until it sinks in.

The true problem dogs in this group are usually very bright and tend to be dominant. Often, these dogs are quite responsive when your trainer handles them, then tune you out entirely. These dogs are limit-testers. Quite literally, they are running a battery of tests on you. They need to determine if you really are Alpha material.

There is a *range* in this group. At one end, we have naturally dominant dogs who test limits sometimes. For example, my Jet has the equivalent of doctoral-level obedience education. If one of my students places her on a down-stay, she will no doubt wait until the student looks away, then belly-crawl out of position, like a solider crawling out of a bunker. She's checking the student out. This is fairly mild limit-testing. We can anticipate that, if not sternly corrected, she will escalate. At the other end of the range, we have dogs engaged in active rebellion. These are dogs who growl when you place them in a down. They're dominant by nature. (Note, however, that some very fearful dogs also will growl when they are handled, in the mistaken belief that they are about to be harmed. They get corrected, too, but with a lighter touch.) Left unchecked, rebellious dogs can develop into true canine terrorists.

The cure is always the same. Fix the dog/owner relationship. These naturally dominant dogs need firm limits and a great deal of affection and praise. A common mistake with the tough guys is to handle them harshly. They do need very firm limits, but they also need to connect with their gentler sides. Teach the dog that obeying your commands and showing respect will earn abundant praise and affection. The breeds we think of as good guard dogs are prone to this kind of dominance. Thus, we see shepherds, Dobermans, rotties and the like being trained with a firm hand, which is good. Too often, though, that's all they get. They need lots of TLC to become good pets. Then you will have not only an alert, powerful dog, but one who will protect you unwaveringly because she loves you so much.

And watch out for the "cute factor." Dog trainer and writer Job Michael Evans warns us about the tendency to not set firm limits on little, adorable dogs. We do it because they're just too cute to scold and we think they're too small to do any real damage. Wrong. Some of the nastiest canine terrorists are cute little dogs. Many small dogs, particularly the terrier breeds, are tough enough to send a Great Dane cowering into a corner. (The Dane probably puts up with it because he thinks the little dog is a puppy and because Danes are such gentle souls.)

So, if your dog has already learned some commands but does what she pleases anyway, it's time to become an Alpha wolf.

OBLIVIOUS DOGS

The first command most trainers teach in a group class is the heel. It's a nice command. The owner no longer has to be dragged down the street. But we have a secret agenda. Teaching the heel requires that the dog pay attention to you. Quite possibly, it will be the first time. When you go to your first group class, watch the dogs as they arrive. They're quite animated and interested. Interested in everything but their owners, that is. With adolescent dogs, it seems it is the natural state of being.

These dogs aren't really bad, they're just clueless. Certainly if you call one of these dogs to "Come!" you can count on the dog's gazing off into the other direction. "Sit!" Who? Me? They may misbehave at home—chewing, digging, running away, whatever. Why not? They really do not know this doesn't please you. From the dog's perspective, you are just another littermate who hangs around in the same den. We often call these dogs stubborn. Entire breeds have been criticized for this sort of thing. A recent article in a dog magazine recommended simply allowing the dog to quit his training exercises when he felt like it. Who's the Alpha in *that* pack?

Some breeds are naturally more aloof and stubborn. That simply means that you will have to work harder to achieve Alphadom. That's all.

Once again, the solution is to work on the relationship between you and your dog. Once the dog learns who the Alpha is, you'll get his attention. Obedience school helps a lot with these dogs. They learn to pay attention, even with lots of distractions.

CANINE ANXIETY

With everything else we have to worry about, now we need to fret about anxious dogs? Anxiety is a bigger problem for dogs than most of us realize. We have forced our dogs to live in a very unnatural world. Veterinarian Michael W. Fox discusses this in *Superdog*. Luckily, the process of domestication has made our pet "wolves" better suited for life in our world than their ancestors would have been.

Trainers often prescribe punishment for common canine capers, like destructive chewing, excessive barking, and other misbehavior considered to be "neurotic." It misses the point.

If your dog is showing these behaviors, the first question to ask is, Does the dog know this doesn't please you?

Okay, you came home, found your rug in pieces, and scolded the dog. So you assume he knows he displeased you. Maybe. Possibly. We used to think that you always had to catch a dog in the act. They're smarter than that. The dog *may* make the connection. Or he may not, depending on the surrounding circumstances. If you're holding up the flotsam that was once a rug and growling at Fido, he just may make the connection. The only sure way is to catch Fido in the act. The problem is, Fido may not be in a good space to hear this feedback. He was stressed enough to do some serious damage. Then the beloved owner finally returned, and he greeted Fido with a menacing growl. Poor Fido's probably not feeling too sure of himself, and the lesson may be lost on him.

Or take the case of Sam, the sweet, docile girl dog who had the nasty habit of attacking visitors. Sam never learned this did not please her owners. After she bit, the owners were understandably shocked and horrified, and all of their attention was focused on the hapless victim. It was not made clear to Sam that her behavior was wrong.

A dog who is being scolded all the time but doesn't know why is a neurotic dog. So your first task is to take a good look at how well the justice system has been operating in your household.

We tend to think like humans. We just sort of assume that *anyone* would know that destroying our belongings is not okay. Your dog really doesn't know this unless you teach him. My impetuous Cassius once plowed his head through a wooden gate that separated the yard from the patio. He disliked artificial boundaries between himself and his humans. So he constructed his own doggy door. Right after he completed this renovation, he beamed at me. He was *proud*. He thought he had done something wonderful.

But how can you teach the dog not to do something if he only does it when you're not there? "Fluffy only wrecks the place when we're at work" is the common theme. Well, Fluffy has lost her right to run the place. Fluffy needs a crate or exercise pen. And Fluffy needs an education. Dogs are pretty consistent. If Fluffy gnaws the furniture while you're gone, she's also going to make a move on it once in a while when the humans are around. Or she'll go after something she shouldn't. She's telling you she hasn't learned yet that these things are off-limits. Keep a sharp eye on her. Confine her to one room where you

can supervise her. In other words, Fluffy needs a second puppyhood. Reread chapter 1, "Puppy Love," and start from scratch.
But suppose you're pretty sure the dog knows his behavior
does not please you. The dog does it anyway. Now what? Step
one is your homework assignment in your Dog Log.

> Start taking notes. Each time the behavior occurs, make some notes
> about what *else* was going on. Especially the feelings of the humans.
> Include facts that may seem irrelevant. Fluffy pooped in the house this
> morning? You may think it's not relevant that you had a dentist appoint-
> ment that day, but write it down anyway. To your dog, everything you
> think, do, and feel is of monumental importance.

If the dog has been driving you crazy, it's okay to lay off for
a while. You've tried every correction in every book and Fido
continues to shred your belongings? Take a break. Crate Fido
and let it go. Get your perspective back. You're probably stressed-
out and frustrated. You'll be able to handle Fido more effectively
once you feel in control again. When Jet suddenly and inexplica-
bly attacked my sheltie, she tore him up pretty badly. I was over
the edge. I loved them both very much. I needed time to sort
things out. I muzzled Jet for a few days. It kept everyone safe
so I could think clearly. Things like crating or extreme measures
like muzzling are short-term emergency measures. They are not
solutions, but stopgaps that allow you to relax and wind down.
That's important, because your own anxiety is going to make
Fido's behavior worse.

BREED-RELATED BEHAVIORS

While you're taking a break from Fido's obnoxious behavior,
read up on Fido's breed. To be fair, we need to sort out what
behaviors could be breed-related. No, it does not let Fido off
the hook. It does give you valuable insights. Fluffy is a Border
collie and you live in a small condo? Fluffy is tearing around
like a banshee, wreaking havoc and destruction? Well, she's a
Border collie. No, they are not bad dogs. They are superb dogs.
Fluffy was bred to work, and work hard. She's an intelligent,

high-energy dog, and a ten-acre working ranch is her idea of heaven. Of course she's wrecking your place. Fluffy's talents are so specific that we sort of have to accommodate her. Fluffy is going to love training, so give her lots of obedience work. Find a herding class. And make sure she gets enough exercise. Wear her out. This is one case where knowing something about your breed really pays off. It would be easy to diagnose Fluffy as hyper or destructive. In reality, she's a perfectly normal, correct Border collie.

You have a terrier who digs holes? Well, of course he does. He's a terrier. Can you fence off an area that the dog can have all to himself so he can dig himself silly? Then teach Fido that the rest of the property is nondiggable. It can be done.

I shudder at the thought of an uneducated German shepherd. Generations of selective breeding went into producing a brilliant workaholic. Then we trainers get calls about shepherds with behavior problems. The owners thought it would be neat to have a German shepherd in the yard to scare burglars away. Or to have a pretty pet. No one should consider this breed unless she or he is completely committed to training. That means working the dog, every single day. Shepherds are not for dilettantes. These dogs were never meant to be house pets. There is, however, no finer working dog than a good, well-educated working line German shepherd. Lots of us trainers own them. They make us look so darned good.

Frankly, there are some breeds that are simply not well suited for life with an inexperienced owner. Some breeds were developed to have strong drives that make them perfect for their specialized careers, but not necessarily good hang-around-the house pets. Shepherds are like this. So are rottweilers and Dobermans. They need good handling and lots of education.

What all this means is, many dogs are living in a state of constant frustration and anxiety. They were bred to do something that we don't want them to do. Some of the most frustrating canine traits actually make perfect sense, once we understand the breed a little better. The scent hounds, for example, are notorious for their stubbornness. Training is a challenge. But think about it. Consider a well-educated bloodhound searching for a lost child. That dog must stay on a trail, unaffected by the presence of dozens of humans, noisy radios, other dogs and while being bombarded by millions of other fascinating smells. We can appreciate that Bloodhound's persistence.

Ever try teaching an Alaskan malamute to walk nicely at heel? Not one of life's easiest tasks. Of course not; the dog was bred to pull a sled. My little sheltie has wonderful manners. But if the humans or other dogs are running around, he yaps up an annoying storm. He needs to herd us. Shelties have so many wonderful qualities, I can live with a little yapping.

Dogdom is full of surprises. Would you love to own a magnificent Great Dane but think he needs forty acres in the country? (Actually, we'd probably all be better off with forty acres in the country.) Believe it or not, the Gentle Giant could thrive in a regular-size yard—provided, of course, you're willing to give the dog sufficient exercise. And a good education. An ill-mannered dog of that size is a menace to all society. Some of these big guys, though, are more laid-back than many smaller breeds. Some of the little terriers can be so high-energy that I'm not sure forty acres would be enough.

GENERIC ANXIETY AND THE PACK DRIVE

Once you've given this some thought and done some reading, you should be able to identify those annoying behaviors which could be breed-related. My yappy little sheltie, for example. Can you rechannel his instincts? I could take my sheltie to herding classes and let him yap himself silly while getting a good workout. A high-energy sporting dog like the Labrador retriever can easily be taught to fetch. He'll have a great time and get the exercise he so desperately needs. So if you have an active, robust family, you've chosen the right dog. Your Lab can take all the fun your kids can dish out. They're sweethearts.

So we see that some canine anxiety can be the result of frustrated drives and instincts. Recall the cooped-up Border collie. She was bred to work tirelessly. No wonder she's a hooligan in a small apartment. But we can work with that. We can find outlets for that energy.

Much canine anxiety is broader-based. It's the net result of making the dog live in our world. Actually, it's the result of making wild wolves into domestic pets.

All dogs, just like the wolves, have basic drives. To properly educate your dog, it's important to understand the power of the pack drive. It's a very underestimated concept. We all pretty much know that dogs are social creatures. They don't appreciate being left alone. We didn't do much to breed pack drive *out* of our dogs. It's a useful trait. It makes the dog loyal and friendly.

But the pack drive goes much deeper than the dog's need for companionship. It is the dog's reason for living. It is the dog's center. To make sense of it, we must go back to our teachers, the wolves.

Wolves survive by capturing and eating prey animals. Their prey of choice is large game: caribou, elk, moose. Think about it: What single wolf would stand a chance of taking down an adult moose? Because of the wolf's predisposition to seek massive, powerful animals for lunch, a wolf has enough sense to hang out with other wolves. This is the origin of the pack drive. Instinctively, the wolf knows he had better stick close to his friends and family. A solitary wolf has virtually no chance to survive. He'll either starve to death or be killed by other predators. The wolf knows this. Hunting is a communal activity.

Pack members bond very deeply. They have to. They need each other; they are completely dependent upon each other. Pack members also develop a powerful attachment to the Alpha. They need him. Again, their survival is at stake. In each pack there is an alpha male as well as an alpha female. Most frequently it is the alpha male who is biggest and strongest and therefore the leader. He represents all the order and security in their world. If the Alpha is here, the wolf thinks, I am safe.

Entire wolf packs have been slaughtered through the trapping of a single wolf. Those wolves died because they were unwilling to abandon a fallen pack member. They paid for their loyalty and devotion with their lives. If you can appreciate this kind of love and loyalty, you are well on your way to being a superior dog owner.

When Mama Wolf needs an outing, pack members are expected to pitch in and care for the pups. The adult wolves,

normally a greedy and voracious lot, will bring back food for
Mama and the baby wolves.

Wolves groom one another. They lick one another's wounds.
They willingly die for one another. It's the power of the pack
drive.

Keeping order in the pack requires a hierarchy. Some wolves
outrank the others. It's the natural order of things. It works for
them. There are plenty of squabbles. Someone will be feeling
his oats (or elk) one day, and throw down a challenge for dominance. There will be lots of noise and posturing. Alphas intervene when they feel they must.

Wolves in a pack maintain constant contact with each other.
They watch. They sniff. If you have two dogs, notice how they
keep an eye on each other. A thorough sniffing may be in order
after being separated for only a few minutes. It's important to
survival. Should one wolf alert on the presence of prey, he must
communicate to the others, quickly. The moose isn't going to
hang around and wait for them to assemble. So wolves stick
close and communicate all the time. A great deal of energy goes
into maintaining pack unity. The pack howl is a call to gather,
a celebration of unity. Wolves love to play. Even senior citizen
wolves remain playful. It keeps the hunting and fighting skills
sharp and promotes pack unity.

Virtually every researcher who has observed a wolf pack has
commented on the wolves' overall *friendliness* toward each other.
Again, it's pure survival instinct. Toward strange wolves, they're
less than hospitable. Your dog knows all about this. He barks at
nonpack members who wander onto pack territory.

The wolf's ability to communicate is phenomenal. Many
students of wolf behavior have referred to wolves as "magical."
I think they are, too. Someday we may have the ability to understand the perceptual abilities of wolves and dogs. For now, we
can call it ESP. Or magic. In *Superdog*, Dr. Fox presents an
interesting discussion of the psychic abilities of animals. Wolves
are highly evolved in the area of perception. Your dog has inherited much of this lupine ESP, or whatever it is. He knows things.

Please, never underestimate the power of the pack drive. *The
pack drive is a fundamental part of the survival instinct.*

On to Fido. What does all this wolf business have to do with him? One night, during a group class, some sirens went by. Predictably, one canine pupil sat, raised his nose in the air, and began to howl. He was quickly joined by several others, my own Thunder-puppy included. It was stirring. My wonderfully aware human students stopped and let them sing. When they were done, I asked my group: "Does anyone still not believe me when I say they are wolves?"

They believed. If you believe, you're halfway to having the dog you want. Fido is not really much different from the precious few wild wolves we have left. He's willing to consider you a pack member. He has the same basic needs and drives.

Consider a typical day for one of our dogs. Each morning, his fellow pack members run off and leave him behind. Poor Fido. In a wolf pack, he would probably get left behind occasionally. That happens. But here, the pack abandons him every single day. He's got to be wondering why. He hates it. He's frustrated. He's anxious. He chews on the forbidden to relieve some tension. It's like lighting up a cigarette. It helps calm him. He's not trying to get even with you. He's trying to cope.

Does this mean your only hope of having a happy dog is to take him with you everywhere? No. Though once he knows a long down-stay, you may want to take him a lot of places. Here's what will save you: Become the Alpha.

Remember the deep trust and respect a wolf feels for the Alpha. Once Fido accepts your Alpha status, he'll have an easier time being left alone. The Alpha gets to make those kinds of decisions, after all. The Alpha's judgment is not open to question. Take it one step further. Give the dog a job to do while you're gone. Leave him with instructions: "Watch the house." "Be a good boy." Here's where so many of us go wrong because we think like humans. We make a big production out of our leaving. We know Fido hates to be alone. We apologize. We beseech poor Fido to leave our belongings alone. We make big promises about the future: "I'll take you to the park when I get home, I *promise*." We negotiate: "If you don't potty in the house today, I'll get you a new toy." We sound totally un-Alpha. Of course Fido doesn't understand the words. He understands the voice only too well. He has a whining Alpha, if he has one at all. How can he have confidence in this Alpha? What guarantees does he have about his safety and well-being?

We go through this elaborate ritual to assuage our own guilt. We discharge a lot of *our* anxiety by verbalizing it. It sends the dogs over the edge, though. Stop doing that. If you feel anxious and guilty about what the dog may feel or do, write it out in your Dog Log instead. Leave the house like a good Alpha. " 'Bye Fido Wolf. Keep an eye on things." Then leave.

Dogs vary in degree of pack drive, but they all have it. Some breeds were bred to be a little more independent. Some are happy only when working in teams. Again, a little research can be a big help. In general though, your dog is driven by his pack drive, which is part of his instinct and will to survive.

So what's the cure for canine anxiety and the host of obnoxious behaviors that go with it? Become a better Alpha. That means inspiring trust in your dog. It also means understanding his natural urge to be part of your pack. Often an owner reports that her dog barks incessantly all night outside. Of course he does. He's bored and lonely and frustrated. His instincts tell him his place is inside with the pack. He's trying to get his owner to listen. More poignantly, he feels it's his responsibility to notify her as to his whereabouts. He honestly believes being left outside all night was an oversight.

There's a catch-22 that comes up all the time: "I can't *let* Rover in the house! He's a maniac, he goes crazy! He'll wreck the place!" Poor Rover. He doesn't have much chance to learn how to behave in the house if he's never allowed inside, does he? Well, even if Rover is seventeen years old, it's time for puppy kindergarten. These owners need to start over from the beginning and raise Rover the right way. Dogs like Rover are usually so thrilled and happy to be in the house, they tolerate crate training just fine.

Lots of us grew up believing that dogs belong outside. Many owners are appalled that I require my students to agree to let the dog live inside with the family as part of their formal education. If you or someone in the household really feels that way, please don't get a dog. It's downright cruel to take nature's most social of creatures and isolate him. Adopt some nice outdoor pet instead. Or maybe some fish. Anything but a dog.

ROOTS

What breed or combination of breeds is your dog? If you're not sure, ask your vet and your trainer.

- What was this breed or breeds developed to do?
- What qualities should a dog have to do this type of work?
- What outlets does your dog have for those natural behaviors?
- What are the negative ways your dog expresses these traits?

You may need to contact a good breeder or consult a breed book to learn about your dog's special roots.

Can you think of any positive ways to channel your dog's natural drives?

Example: Sissy, a two-year-old Jack Russell terrier. Developed to capture and kill vermin. JRTs are exceptionally high in hunting instinct, high even for a terrier. To be good at this, Sissy should be quick, agile, and fearless and have a high prey drive. Current outlets include tearing around the house, climbing all over everything, and trying to run away. The negatives include all of the above, plus the fact that she is totally untrustworthy off-leash, is a perpetual motion machine, and has shown aggression when she does not get her own way.

Positive outlets: Agility classes! The sport of agility was probably invented by a Jack Russell. They *love* it. They get to sprint over an obstacle course while being timed. Of course, Sissy will need to be obedience-trained first, but agility is absolutely custom made for this little dog. Wear this dog out doing things she loves to do: running and jumping and exploring.

Tracking is another good outlet for Sissy, and a good way to get her tired.

THE RESISTANCE MOVEMENT

Many dog owners are taken aback when they read my enrollment agreement and get to the clause that says the dog will be allowed to sleep in the house with the family. What? A dog in the house? What heresy!

If the dog is forced to be isolated from the pack, especially at bedtime, do not expect the dog's behavior to improve. Why should he care what the humans want when he has been so cruelly rejected?

If your dog has been one of those outdoor dogs, make a list of reasons why:

- He might go potty in the house.
- He might wreck something.
- It's not healthy [for whom?]
- Dog prefers it.
- Dirt.
- Spouse or other household member objects.

These are the most common objections. None of them are good ones, however.

The Potential Potty Problem is fixable: housebreak the dog. As for wrecking things, get a crate to keep the dog confined until proper household etiquette has been taught. The health concerns are a mystery; people don't catch dog diseases and vice versa. They're a different species.

As for the dog's preferring it, that's ludicrous. No dog prefers to be separated from her family. In these households, the dog who seems to be willingly staying outside is merely complying with the owners' wishes. She actually hates it, but is committed to pleasing her owners, no matter how unreasonable their demands.

Dirt? That's the easiest fix around. Keep the dog well groomed, so he sheds less. Wipe mud off his paws. Invest in a better vacuum cleaner.

If another household member objects, get to the bottom of it. What is the basis of the objection? Is it fixable? It usually is. With a truly resistant spouse, do not underestimate the power of the long down-stay. Get your dog bombproof on that down-stay. Even non–dog people have a tough time objecting to the presence of a dog on down-stay. It

dazzles them. The long down-stay is responsible for many, many dogs-
sleeping in the house tonight. Once the down-stay champion impresses
everyone enough, household members just may find themselves bonding
to the dog, in spite of themselves.

 MORE ROOTS

Keeping in mind that all dogs, even the little cutie pies, are domesticated
wolves, what is a "wolfie" thing you have seen your dog do? Some
examples:

A friend told me she saw Jet drop a chewy into a large trough of
water. Jet then proceeded to try sticking her paw in the water and
grabbing at it until she caught it. She looked exactly like videos my
friend had seen of a wolf catching a fish.

Thunder, normally not a voracious eater, found a dead, rotting gopher
(it was decomposing to the point of liquifying). He proceeded to dine
on it with great gusto until I caught him.

CHAPTER FIVE
Corrections

We trainers get calls all the time about Behavior Problems: "My dog jumps up on people. What can I do?" Trainers, unfortunately, often prescribe "corrections." For jumping up, get a water bottle and squirt the dog in the face. Many dogs have learned to enjoy the "water game." Some trainers continue to prescribe the use of a "throw can." This is an aluminum soda can (no one ever suggests using a beer can) that has been rinsed out (very important) and contains twelve pennies (count them carefully, it doesn't work with eleven). The idea is to toss the can at the dog when the dog is misbehaving. The sound is supposed to startle the dog. It's as ridiculous as it sounds. These trainers endorse the throw can for everything. I have no idea why. They claim it's better if the dog thinks the correction came from the "environment" rather than from you. Why? And do they think your dog is stupid enough to fall for that? That the dog believes there is some cosmic can-thrower hovering about just waiting for him to act up? No! The dog knows perfectly well you threw a soda can at him. There is nothing in the collective canine unconscious that tells them Alpha wolves do this sort of thing. It's silly. It makes you look silly. You want your dog to know darn good and well from whence all corrections come. They come from the Alpha wolf, which is something your dog instinctively understands and accepts.

Owners seek obedience training because they want the dog to learn the rules and obey. What we're failing to realize is that dogs *already are following the rules.* The rules are set forth in the Pack Code, which all dogs instinctively know and obey. A dominant dog is telling the owner, quite clearly, that she did not have the right to disturb him on the bed. He feels he can do this because he fancies himself the Alpha in their pack. His behavior is consistent with the Pack Code.

Does that mean we have to tolerate this sort of behavior? Of course not. But it's more useful to recognize that we cannot address behavior problems in isolation. We're always looking for the "magic correction" for whatever problem we're having with the dog. There isn't one. Some tricks work for a while, others backfire, like the "water game." Other times, the dog finds a new way to express himself. Perhaps lifting his leg in the house.

To return to the jumping-up question: Dogs jump on people for more than one reason. Some dogs do it as a display of dominance. Others are showing affection, even submission. It may be an attempt to face-lick, another wolf throwback. Juvenile wolves face-lick in hopes that the adult will provide some regurgitated food. The behavior hangs on in some dogs as a submissive greeting. Does that mean you have to let your dog jump up on you? Absolutely not. So what's the "correction"? The same as for all problems: Become the Alpha. Educate the dog. Once you have taught the dog to sit on command, you can give her an alternative to jumping up as a greeting. Fluffy jumps up? "NOOOOO! Fluffy, sit!" Now give her the petting and greeting she wants. If Fluffy's jumping up was a dominance display, establishing Alpha status will go a long way toward stopping her. If she's just showing affection, she can learn that sitting nicely elicits petting and praise more efficiently than jumping on you.

CORRECTIONS

Make a list of the old tried-and-true corrections you have used in the past that didn't work.

With your new understanding of the canine perspective, explain why didn't the correction work.

Example: We tried the old knee-in-the-chest punishment to break our yellow Lab, Sassy, from jumping up all the time. It didn't work at all; in fact, she got worse.

Why it didn't work: One of the things we've learned about Labs is that they are very friendly, and they just love body contact. So when we gave Sassy a knee in the chest, she loved it. She thinks it's a wrestling game.

See how far you have come already? Now you know those outdated, quick-fix corrections don't work, and you also understand why they don't work.

ALPHA SCHOOL

By now you know why we call our facility the Silver Wolf Academy. It's a tribute to the real experts on canine behavior. And it's a constant reminder of who our pupils really are. A good obedience school should really be called the Alpha Academy. The goal is to teach you to be a good Alpha wolf, after all.

The first thing you must learn to do is *growl* properly. This does not come naturally to most humans. Learn to deliver a deep, menacing "NOOOOOOOOOO!" Add a very stern glare. With most dogs, a really impressive growl and glare is the sternest correction you will ever need. When I demonstrate a growl to a new group of students, every dog in the place will stop what he's doing and look at me. That's all the feedback I need. Of course, if unenlightened humans hear you, they'll think you're nuts. Learn to ignore them. It's an Alpha thing to do.

So, how do you know if you're growling properly? Does your dog instantly stop what she's doing and look up at you? You're on the right track. If her ears are pinned back, you really got through. To gauge human growling effectiveness, I developed the Construction Crew Test.

A client had a young Airedale terrier who was bolting out

the front door and crossing the street to superintend a construction site. Her owner was justifiably worried that she'd be hit by a car, so we commenced boundary training. After some time getting her used to working with fifty feet of clothesline attached to her collar, we took the dog outside and placed her in a sit-stay. Predictably, she started to amble off toward the street. I grabbed her by the collar with my best Alpha growl: "NOOOOO!" The entire construction crew shut down, hopped off their equipment, and turned to see what creature had made that horrendous sound.

That's the standard by which growls should be judged. If your growl was sufficiently menacing to stop a construction crew in its tracks, it was a good growl. Needless to say, the Airedale was not anxious to leave the yard after that. Her owner continued to work with her. That correction was pretty melodramatic. Running into the street is life-threatening behavior and strong corrections are entirely reasonable. Also, the dog had been through Basic Obedience, so we held her to a higher standard than an uneducated dog.

Don't worry. You won't have to spend the rest of your life making a public spectacle. Once your dog is properly educated and has learned to respect your authority, you'll be able to tone down the dramatic intensity of your corrections. A well-educated dog often requires little more than a dirty look to get her back into line.

Follow-through is also important. Once you have growled and the dog stopped what she was doing, PRAISE, PRAISE, PRAISE. You must shift gears and use your most animated, happy voice: "Goooood Dooooog!" You're signaling to the dog that stopping the incorrect behavior was exactly what you wanted and you are just delighted with her. Never forget the praise part. Be effusive and go crazy with it. Be generous with your praise. The more heartfelt it is, the faster the dog will learn.

So if your dog is one of the many who simply doesn't understand, start communicating with her in ways that make sense to the dog.

How do you know how you're doing? You'll get plenty of feedback from your dog. Is she gazing at you adoringly? Does he seem to feel the need to be near you at every opportunity? Most of all, is the dog's behavior improving?

If the dog isn't shaping up, it may be time to evaluate your corrections. You've growled like an Alpha and glared menacingly. Maybe you even delivered a good scruff-shaking, a technique your dog's mother perfected. How do you know if it worked? Job Michael Evans has said that one well-timed, good correction will save you dozens of ineffective, demoralizing poor corrections. One really strong correction may look and sound bizarre, but if it got through, it may be all you ever need.

If the dog went right back to whatever canine caper she was engaged in, it's safe to say you missed your mark. If she bounces around, thinking the whole thing was really funny, she didn't get it. The appropriate response is a very shaken-up pooch. My Cash had a look that was unmistakable. His giant radar ears went flat against his head and he would just *slink* down the nearest wall. He then would place himself on a down-stay (he was confident the Alpha liked those) for thirty minutes or so. He would look over at me every few minutes. I'd ignore him, which was precisely what he expected an Alpha to do. We Alphas have the right to ignore subordinates, remember? It's an assertion of social dominance. Cash was always so completely humiliated by the entire ordeal that he learned to avoid getting corrections. It was worth it to him.

If you're not getting through, increase the dramatic intensity of your corrections. *This does not include hitting your dog.* Ever! Some training books have prescribed giving the dog a good cuff under the chin, for serious misconduct. Well, it's reasonably safe. Your hand is no match for a canine jaw that can exert about a thousand pounds per square inch. You can't hurt the dog this way. The problem is, it doesn't work. Hitting makes absolutely no sense to any dog. His mother never hit him, no matter how obnoxious he got as a puppy. Growl, glare, scruff-shake, roll over and pin, sure. But hit? Never. The collective canine unconscious can't make heads or tails out of hitting.

When the Cassusaurus first joined my pack, I quickly came to suspect that his former owners had relied on the old rolled-up-newspaper-on-the-nose form of discipline. If Cash saw me with a newspaper or magazine in my hand, he cowered and cringed. It scared him. He was head-shy about it. It made him want to get away from me, not obey me. Eventually he learned we don't do things that way and he got over it. I didn't want my new dog to be afraid of me. Nor did I want to give up reading.

Hitting a dog is abusive. It will do nothing to make her respect you. Use corrections she can understand. If you're not getting through, you may have to be more theatrical. Keep in mind, the Alpha controls the pack with a lot of *posturing*. It looks and sounds impressive. There are bloodcurdling snarls. Dogs love this high drama. It makes sense to them. If Fluffy persists in gnawing the furniture despite your best growl, growl harder. And longer. Stand up and tower over Fluffy. Let her know that she is a complete menace to society. Make a dreadful racket. Don't forget, the second she backs off from the gnawing, PRAISE HER EFFUSIVELY. It seems crazy to humans, but dogs do shift emotional gears that quickly. Okay, no harm done. All's forgiven.

This is an important concept in working with your dog: NO GRUDGES! Remember the big dog with the recalcitrant puppy? Big Dog disciplined the puppy with a fine snarl. Big Dog then got over it. Instantly. He didn't take the puppy's behavior personally. The adult sees misbehavior and corrects it, swiftly and sternly. Then it is over. They can play now. It takes hard work for us humans to learn this. We get caught up in humanizing our dogs' motivations.

"Well, see, usually we take Fluffy to the park on Saturday, but last Saturday we couldn't because I had to work. So on Monday, when I got home from work, I knew she was really mad at me about not going to the park, because she pooped in the house and she chewed up my brand-new shoes." Really? Fluffy is a genius! She actually knew when it was Saturday, was able to restrain herself till Monday, and then let her owner have it?

Here's what really happened: Fluffy didn't have a clue that it was Park Day. She may very well have picked up that her owner was acting weird, though. She's a body language professional, after all. Monday morning rolled around and the owner felt bad about leaving Fluffy alone all day. Fluffy's thinking: Hmm. Something's odd around here. I wonder what's wrong with my owner. She may have become anxious enough to get destructive. Wonder what the good-bye scene was like on Monday? "Ooooh, Fluffy, I'm so sorry, I have to leave you. Be a good girl for Mommy, okay? Pleeeese? I promise I'll take you to the park next Saturday, I really will. . . ." Good grief. Fluffy is one psychologically stable dog or she would have had a complete nervous breakdown by now.

Or possibly Fluffy's owner was just seething at the boss for making her work on Saturday. Do you think your dog doesn't know these things? Your dog knows how you *feel*, believe me. What she has trouble with is making sense of it. Dogs live in the here and now. If you're furious at someone, Fluffy knows it. She assumes she's the one you're mad at. When two humans argue, often the poor dog will run under the nearest table. Dogs don't like this sort of thing. It scares them. They expect the Alpha to protect them. Disharmonious human relationships really affect our dogs.

Okay, it's not a perfect world. We get mad at our human companions. We have bad days. Well, no one is suggesting you get a divorce for the benefit of your dog (though it's been known to happen). Dogs are like emotional weather vanes for us. They miss nothing. We can't hide our feelings from them. Just try to keep in mind that your emotional well-being is important to your dog. Learning some stress management will be good for both of you. If things get really out of control at home, let Fluffy spend some time in her crate. A secure, cozy den will help her stress management.

Owners often do well with their dogs, learn to growl properly, and get frustrated because the dog misbehaves when the owner's not around. They incorrectly assume the dog is acting out of spite. Dogs don't. They do misbehave out of anxiety, at times. Dogs chew on furniture in large part because they are dogs. They have to learn not to. The treatment for anxious dogs is to get that dog working. Regular obedience work helps many dogs calm down and focus.

If Fluffy is tearing up the house while the owner is away, Fluffy is going to have to give up having the freedom to tear up the house. She may have to be crated or penned until she settles down. This is a tough one. You cannot keep Fluffy in her crate for eight hours at a time. Can you come home for lunch and let her out? Is there a responsible kid in the neighborhood you can hire to take Fluffy out for a walk while you're at work?

Yes, it's a hassle. Owning a dog requires a lifestyle change for most of us. It's not realistic to lock the dog up in the house for ten hours a day and expect your belongings to be intact. The dog gets frustrated and anxious. With enough exercise and a full-time job, the dog can learn to stay home and behave herself while you're gone. She needs plenty of physical and mental stimulation first.

If you're truly committed to owning a dog, you'll find a way. When I first adopted my sheltie, many years ago, I did it because I simply could not live without a dog in my life any longer. I was working full-time and going to school full-time, three or four nights a week. I lived in student-type studio apartments. A sheltie was a good choice. Shelties can adapt to life in small spaces with no undue hardship. Before we got a place with a fenced yard, our typical day went something like this: Up at the crack of dawn to walk Noël. (Eventually I was able to hop in the shower while still asleep and let my hair dry while on our walk.) Then, off to the office, downtown. After work, straight home to play a rousing game of fetch for fifteen to thirty minutes. Then back downtown for class. Three hours later, home to Noël for his evening stroll and some quality time. I missed lots of Happy Hours. There were a lot of student bashes I didn't go to, because I wanted to get home to Noël. Being a sheltie, Noël took it all in stride. Saturdays were our day. We took long, long walks in the park, or visited friends. Sundays, we just sort of hung out together. It all worked out just fine.

 CREATIVE SOLUTIONS

Borrow a technique used by big corporations. Tackle the seemingly un-solvable problems. Brainstorm, *without* censoring. Write all of your stream-of-consciousness ideas in your Dog Log, even if they seem off-the-wall. Many, many brilliant ideas have been hatched this way.

Example: My husband and I both work full-time and have very long commutes, over an hour each way. Fang has been destroying the house while we're gone.

Possible solutions:

- Both quit our jobs and stay home with Fang.
- Sell the house and move closer to work.
- Look into telecommuting.
- Talk to our dog-owning friends, what are they doing? Is there such a thing as a doggie day care? Could we get together and start one? Do we know any stay-at-home moms who could be bribed into service?
- Talk to the neighbor's nice kid. We know she does a lot of baby-sitting. Could she do dog walking? Dog playing?
- Pay the local boarding kennel to keep Fang during the day.
- Build a bombproof dog run.
- Fence the yard. (It'll increase the value of the property anyway.) Then we could get a playmate for Fang.
- Change our work schedules.
- Get up earlier and take Fang for a good run, since a tired dog is a good dog (after a visit to the vet for an appropriate conditioning program).

As you can see, even an "unsolvable" problem can generate a number of ideas. When I do behavior counseling, I can quickly distinguish the owners who should have dogs from the ones who probably should not. Some owners are full of "yes, buts." "Yes, but we'd have to pay the neighbor's daughter and we can't afford it," they insist, before they've even talked to the neighbor. Perhaps the kid wouldn't ask for a fortune; or there is a service you could swap. Maybe she needs some work on her car and your husband is a genius mechanic. Creativity will get you much further than the "Yes, but . . ." philosophy. "Yes, but" owners contact me for advice, but what they really want is for me to agree with them. Yes, you're right, the situation is completely hopeless, it is not your fault and there is nothing you can do about it.

Really good, committed owners, on the other paw, really get into the problem-solving game. The owner of a darling, active little golden re-triever puppy got creative, with spectacular results. He talked to his neighbors. He found a responsible young lady who wanted to come over during the afternoons and play with the puppy. She was *thrilled* with the idea and would gladly have paid my client for the privilege. He went a step further. He taught the young girl how to do the puppy obedience lessons, including the Follow Game. Then, he built a truly bombproof, large dog run to spare his lawn and garden. The puppy's day is broken up by the visit from her young friend; they train, they play, and they walk. The owner works with the dog when he gets home from his job, and takes her for long walks. The result: no more destructive behavior. The puppy has a lot to do and plenty to look forward to. Everybody won. The puppy is happier, the owner is happier, and the young neighbor is getting excellent handling experience and learning about responsible pet ownership.

So if you have an especially vexing behavior problem, do some creative brainstorming. And watch out for that "Yes, but . . ."

Eventually we got a fenced yard and life became much easier. Noël could take himself out at the crack of dawn. Lots of us learn to open the door and let the dog out into the yard without ever waking up. These are the adjustments we humans have to make when we decide to get a dog. I never for a second have thought it wasn't worth it.

When I finally finished school, I found a place in the city with a third of an acre, fully fenced. The sky was the limit now! I could have my dream dog, a German shepherd. That's when Jet joined the pack and my real education began.

USE OF FORCE

We've talked about a few wolf/Mama Dog corrections. They don't look a thing like the traditional rolled-up newspaper. There's generally plenty of growling (on our part) and lots of melodrama. If you have delivered a good, theatrical correction, did you notice your dog's reaction? He was certainly not enjoying himself, but you should have seen a certain recognition, an acceptance. That's because the correction was delivered in a way that made sense to the dog.

Our goal is *never* to cause injury or physical pain to a dog.

That's animal abuse. This is why your acting skills are so important: displeasing the Alpha leads to social mortification, not physical harm. Hitting your dog will make him want to escape you, not respect you. And, it's an efficient way to create a biting dog.

Accept the fact that discipline does require some force. Your dog's mother did it beautifully. But how much is too much? Some dogs are more hardheaded than others. Some canine crimes are more heinous than others. And some owners are more anxious about the whole affair than others. As a rule, you want to use the least amount of force that is effective.

The best model for explaining the use of force is stolen directly from the police academies. These are really Alpha Academies; good cops are very Alpha.

When a police officer turns on her red light and signals you to pull over, what do you do? No doubt you curse under your breath, but you probably stop your car. Why? Because you saw the patrol car and the uniform. That's the cop's "command presence." Just by being there, the police have a certain amount of power over us. It's the lowest level of force available to them.

When the officer asks for your license and registration, she probably says something like, "I need to see your license and registration. Please." She does *not* say something like, "Excuse me, but if it's not too much trouble, I really hate to bother you, but would you mind terribly, I know it's an inconvenience, but would it be okay if I looked at your driver's license for just one second?" As you can see, even we law-abiding types would have trouble taking the cop in the second example very seriously. She's not Alpha. Giving you a verbal command is the next level of force the cop can use. Many, many owners sound exactly like the un-Alpha cop when they discipline their dogs.

Most of us don't challenge police officers when they stop us, so the use of force doesn't escalate. Suppose, however, the driver has refused to comply. The officer can direct him out of the vehicle, for her own safety. She can search him for weapons. She can even physically remove him from the car, if need be. You can see how a confrontation can escalate. Other officers will appear to help the first cop. If an officer is threatened, weapons will be drawn. The subject may find himself in handcuffs. The whole thing will just keep going until the subject figures out that the cops are the ones running the show.

It's a lot like this with your dog. Once your dog is well educated and recognizes your Alpha status, your mere command presence will be enough to keep him in line. My Cash is like this. It generally doesn't take more than a stern look or a "Cash!" to get him to stop misbehaving. Some dogs aren't paying attention to you because they haven't gotten it through their heads that you are the one in charge. You may have to get their attention by grabbing a collar or scruff and forcing eye contact. Does the dog try to squirm away, avoiding eye contact? This is the guy who wouldn't let the cop see his driver's license. He's not getting the picture. The dog who gazes into your eyes with a look of recognition and then looks respectfully away does get the picture. Immediately after the correction is when you'll know if it got through. It's like the cop who writes a speeding ticket and sends you on your way. If she sees you peeling out and racing away at 85 mph, she knows you didn't quite get the message. If the dog goes right back to his canine caper, you didn't get through.

When you deliver a proper, well-deserved correction, you should get a shaken-up, humble pooch. Suppose, for example you catch Fluffy in the act of gnawing on the furniture: "NOOOOO!" you growl, menacingly. Fluffy now must make amends. She must cease and desist. A truly respectful dog will offer up an appeasement gesture. Do her ears go back, and her head go down? She's trying to look smaller, which is a canine form of apologizing. Or does she go right back to the gnawing? Now's the time to escalate! Give her your most fearsome growl, and grab some scruff. Remember, the instant she lets go of the chair leg, she gets her PRAISE. If Fluffy has a stubborn streak, you'll have to be more melodramatic. As soon as the dog offers you a show of appeasement, PRAISE HER UP. Your goal is not to demoralize and terrorize the dog. If she's been really bratty, give her a long down-stay, to cement-in your correction and clear up any doubts she may be entertaining about your relative rankings in the hierarchy.

At the police academy, recruits are taught to use psychology rather than raw force whenever possible. It's safer. Attitude really is everything. Have you developed sufficient command presence with your dog? If not, spend more time on the obedience work, especially the long down-stay.

What corrections weapons do you get to keep in your arsenal? You're limited to those that your dog can make sense of. Growling in the most theatrical and menacing way possible is an awesome correction tool. Grabbing the scruff and forcing eye contact is the next logical step. Rolling Fido over and pinning him is a powerful, but grossly misused, technique.

THE ROLLOVER

New dog owners keep telling me they were told to do "dominance training." The advice came from the vet, or the trainer. What they're told to do is roll the dog over and pin her, several times a day. Don't do this!

The rollover correction is reserved for *extremely serious misbehavior only*. It mimics a dominant wolf disciplining a subordinate. The dominant one rolls the dog over, onto her back, keeping one paw on the subordinate's throat. Lots of growling and glaring go with it. The technique requires supreme confidence and sure timing. It's an easy way to get bitten.

Using the roll over for minor infractions terrorizes the dog. Some experts are prescribing rolling the new dog (or puppy!) over and pinning *five times a day*. It guarantees a neurotic dog.

The rollover is an effective correction tool. All dogs instinctively understand it. It puts them in their place, rather melodramatically. It does not hurt the dog physically, but it has a profound psychological effect. The dog won't be quite the same again.

If your dog has a serious aggression problem, the rollover may be inevitable. Don't even attempt it until you have obedience-trained your dog, and become an experienced handler. If it fails, you'll have a much worse dog than you started with. You've got to be physically up to pulling this off, in one smooth, coordinated motion. If you haven't already established dominance over the dog, through training, it will backfire completely. The dog will learn you are not Alpha. It's the wrong lesson.

The importance of timing can't be emphasized too strongly. This correction is just not for casual use. Done right, it's extraordinarily effective. Done wrong, it's guaranteed disaster.

After I'd been working with Jet for several weeks following her attack on my sheltie, the opportunity presented itself. Jet was in the kitchen, starting her Dominant Dog Swagger. As she put a paw on Noël's back, I got her. She found herself on her back, on the kitchen floor, gazing up at a very noisy Alpha. Jet is such a dominant dog that she struggled fiercely for several minutes while I held her down. At last, It happened: She gazed into my eyes with a look of complete, total recognition. She relaxed. She properly turned her eyes away from mine. She accepted it. I kept her in position for several more minutes.

Cash provided the comic relief. He watched from outside, peering through the sliding glass door. The look on his expressive face was complete horror. His ears were glued to his head. He was hoping that never happened to him. (It never did.)

When I finally released Jet, she ran outside and snarled at Cassius. She was upset. She had lost face in the most degrading manner. She had to take it out on somebody, other than Noël. Cash knew how to appease her. He wasn't about to accept her challenge to brawl. No way was he going to displease his Alpha and get himself rolled over.

That was probably the best-timed, most effective correction I've ever delivered. I don't use the rollover often. Keep in mind that this was several weeks into Jet being on Tough Love. She was being put through her paces several times a day. She had to "sit" or "down" to get any attention from me. She was ripe for that kind of correction. It reinforced the obedience work we were doing, and sent the clear message: I am Alpha. You will not pick on the little dog.

Jet stayed away from me for an hour or so. This is an entirely correct response. She knew she'd fallen far from favor with the Alpha and had no right to solicit attention. When she finally did approach, it was with great humility. This is why we don't do the rollover for minor misdemeanors. She was deeply affected. Her dignity was gone. She was one humble pup. I don't want to bring a dog to her knees over the small stuff. This was to correct serious aggression. She had nearly killed my little sheltie. I had received two bites from her over the years. She was a dangerous dog. I had already decided that if I couldn't train the aggression out of her, she would have to be euthanized. She certainly couldn't be placed in another home. Her life, literally, was at stake. That's a good time to pull out all the stops.

Also, Jet was thoroughly obedience-trained. She knew the rules. She made the choice, then and there, to live with the pecking order as it was. She could be dominant over the other dogs, but she had to respect her Alpha.

Jet's behavior shaped up after that. We still had plenty of work to do, but she became a more respectful dog. She started looking for ways to please me. Luckily for her, this is easy to do. She can do excellent sits and downs. She can do a long stay. Instead of whacking me with a paw when she wanted something, she started sitting, ears way back, in front of me.

So please don't get caught up in this new fad, wherever it came from, of "dominance training." If you're doing obedience work and being a good Alpha, your dog is learning you are dominant. Don't terrorize and demoralize the dog. Save the heavy artillery for serious misbehavior. And use it only after everything else has failed.

But keep in mind, corrections can only take you so far. You must at the same time be working on your relationship with your dog. Obedience lessons and generous praise for good behaviors will correct your dog's behavior much more effectively than any discipline techniques.

The next time your dog is acting up, stop and listen to yourself. Do you sound like the Alpha cop? Are you behaving in an Alpha-like manner?

TOUGH LOVE

 DOMINANCE TRAINING THE RIGHT WAY

List some positive ways in which you are teaching your dog that you outrank him. For example:

- Taught Rover a little routine he has to do before we give him his supper dish or a treat. He has to come, sit, and down before we feed him.
- Taught Rover a "Wait!" command; he must wait in the doorway while I go out first and he cannot exit until given the "Okay!" release.

Can you think of still more that would make good dogsense?

If your dog's behavior is really driving you crazy, it's time for Tough Love. The underlying theme of the program is that the free ride is over. Privileges must be earned from this moment forward. The dog is a dog, and by definition, subordinate to humans. You've been behaving like a proper Alpha for a while now, but the dog still isn't taking you seriously. Here is the program in a nutshell:

1. Daily obedience lessons, ten minutes, twice a day. Every day, including rainy days, holidays, and lunar eclipses.
2. The dog is not allowed on *any* furniture.
3. At mealtime, the dog must sit nicely before his dish will be placed in front of him.
4. The dog is served after the humans dine.
5. NO TREATS. No kidding.
6. Owner engages in Alpha Manuevers: you go through doorways first; you wake sleeping dogs and direct them to "MOVE!" in your best Alpha voice. If the dog fails to move, you push him out of your way. You do not step over snoozing pooches. Alphas have these rights and your dog knows it.
7. No outings. (Except obedience school or the vet.)
8. If the dog is not in the process of following a command, he is not on the planet. No gratuitious petting. If you must pet the dog, make him earn it by sitting or downing first.
9. The dog will be wearing a buckle (not a chain) collar and a short leash indoors. Never be out of position to enforce a command or give a correction. If he's totally

out of control, crate him when you can't watch every move he makes.

10. No chattering at the dog. Address him to give commands and praise. Enjoy his quiet companionship.

The dog has fallen to the position of Pack Outcast. Don't give in to feelings of sympathy. This is for his own good. Nothing hurts a dog more than falling out of favor with the Alpha. Make it clear he must earn his way back into the pack. You'll need to stay with the program for at least thirty days for it to be effective.

Most training books will insist that everyone in the household must be consistent in dealing with the dog. In a perfect world, that's what would happen. In real life, it never does. Somebody in the household is going to feel sorry for Fido and let him on the bed, or slip him a treat. What's a good owner to do? Stay with the program. What generally happens is Fido shapes up and bonds to the one who behaved in the most Alpha-like way. The rest of the household may continue to have problems with him, but he'll learn to respect you, as his true Alpha. He'll consider the rest of the human pack his littermates and no doubt treat them accordingly. Oh, well.

Let's look at each of the tenets of the program. The daily obedience lessons are mandatory. Fido needs a job and a way to get attention from you that is in both of your best interests. Ten-minute sessions prevent boredom and burnout from setting in. Always end the lesson on a happy note, even if you have to go back to a command he learned long ago. Reward him with a short play session with you. Give him something to look forward to.

We're not keeping the dog off the furniture to punish him. Dogs love the furniture. It's comfy. The problem is, being on the furniture puts the dog physically on the same plane with the humans. It makes him your social equal. That's the wrong message, at the moment. Later, when he is respectful and well-mannered, you can allow him back on. It's not going to last forever.

Fido never gets to eat first. In the wild, the Alpha male and female get first pickings. The subordinates must wait and accept leftovers. If you feed Fido first, what can he think except that he outranks you?

Of course, Fido gets *nothing* for free anymore. Naturally, he must sit for his supper. It sends him exactly the right message.

What about treats? Why the no-treats policy? Most dogs with behavior problems are overtreated. Dominant dogs really use this against their owners. They actually demand, and get, treats. Or the owner falls into the trap of bribing the dog into good behavior: "I had to give him a biscuit so he wouldn't run out the gate." That is bad news. Fido can live a long and healthy life without treats. Again, once his behavior improves, he can enjoy a biscuit now and then, at the *Alpha's* whim.

Certainly the dog shouldn't be getting *any* human food. It's bad for dogs and can create behavior problems. If your dog is on a premium-quality dry feed, he's doing just fine. Adding tidbits will throw the whole system out of balance and do no good whatsoever. If you really need to feel good about doing something nice for your dog, take him for a walk instead. It's a great way to practice the heel.

Practice being an Alpha. Little things mean a lot to a dog. Dogs will resort to violence over who goes out the door first because the highest-ranking pack member has this privilege. Your dog knows this. Stepping over or around a sleeping dog is subordinate behavior, since Alphas have an absolute right to go where they please. Wake your dog up and make him move out of your way. He may not like it, but you're racking up lots of dog status points. All of these seemingly insignificant gestures have powerful meanings to canine minds. Use them to your advantage.

By "no outings" we mean no gratuitous rides to the supermarket and everyplace else Fido thinks he should go. That does not mean canceling his daily exercise walks in the park. But if your dog has gotten into the habit of going with you on errands, he just may have gotten spoiled. Consider this case of the busy owners. Both spouses have full-time jobs. They took their vacation time at home. Their two mixed-breed dogs got to go *everywhere* with their owners. Even a quick trip to the drugstore meant a ride in the truck. This went on for a full week. When the owners returned home after their first day back at work, the house was in shambles. The dogs had come to expect to be included in everything and had major anxiety attacks at being left behind.

If the dog is not in the process of following a command, he is not on the planet, because dominant dogs are experts at *demanding* attention from the humans and you need to short-circuit this. Alphas do not respond to demands for attention, petting, or games. Many dogs with behavior problems are fussed over too much. They never learn their place in the hierarchy. It doesn't take much extra effort to direct Fido to sit before he gets the petting he wants. Eventually, Fido will approach you and place himself in a sit when he wants attention. What a delightful day that will be!

Try to eliminate excess petting for the duration of the program. It mimics the behavior of subordinate canids toward their social superiors. That's not the message you want to send.

Keeping the dog on leash indoors is the way to manage truly out-of-control canines. Does she run around and get into everything and drive everyone crazy? Well, now she can't. Nor will you find yourself giving commands that are ignored.

Remember what we've already learned about canine communication: Human chattering sounds like *whining*. Alphas do not whine. Littermates whine. Constantly chatting at the dog only confuses him. Use your voice to issue instructions, correct, and praise. The dog needs to learn to pay attention to your voice. He won't do that if he hears it constantly. If you spend some time quietly hanging out with your dog and just observing him, you will find yourself learning a great deal.

 PLAN B

When you commence your program for correcting a serious problem behavior, it helps to have a Plan B as a backup. For example, you resolve to correct Rover's destructive chewing. You'll be:

- Starting him on daily obedience lessons, to reduce his anxiety and gain more control over his behavior.

- Supervising him diligently in the house.
- Providing appropriate chew toys.
- Keeping your arrivals and departures low-key.
- And if all else fails, you can always [you fill in the blank].

In Rover's case, keep a crate or a pen handy as a backup. So if you aren't getting through to Rover, you can always crate him when you can't supervise his every move.

Why is the Plan B important? Because you're taking control of the situation and your peace of mind will increase. When your anxiety drops, Rover's will, too. You may never have to use the crate, but you'll be glad it's there. (They're easy to resell, by the way. People always need crates.)

CHAPTER SIX

The ABCs

Your dog needs and deserves a good education. That includes obedience training. Training is only part of a good education. The dog has a lot to learn beyond basic commands. The dog must learn his position in the pack. And he must learn to respect the Alpha in his life. I'm always appalled at trainers who advertise the number of dogs they have trained ("Over eight thousand dogs trained!"). The only dogs I have ever trained are my own. I have, however, educated many owners. Any halfway competent trainer can teach a dog some basic commands. But what happens when the dog goes home?

That's why the emphasis must always be on owner education. You are the one who is going to educate your dog.

GETTING STARTED

Okay. You have decided to be a good Alpha wolf. You are going to take over where your dog's mother left off and educate him. Just how, exactly, do you start?

Every trainer teaches commands differently. That's okay. We all have our own style. Here are a few basic rules to keep in mind, for maximum results:

1. Never issue a command unless you are in a position to enforce it. Don't tell Fido to sit from across the room. Every time you give a command and the dog gets away with ignoring it, you'll have to work ten times harder. There is no federal, state, or municipal ordinance that bans you from having a leash on your dog indoors. You may need to do this in the beginning if Fido is really out of control.

2. Always use the same command for the same behavior.

3. Issue a command ONCE. If you direct Fluffy to sit and she fails to place her hindquarters on the ground at once, you do it for her. Fluffy does not need to learn a command called "Sit, sit, sit, I told you to sit!" Besides, you don't sound very Alpha.

4. Corrections should be quick and clean. Timing is an art. There should be no lag time between the misbehavior and the correction. It's not fair to the dog to make him think backward.

5. Use lots of praise. Praise your dog each and every time a command is carried out, *even if you had to do it for him*. For now, the dog needs to associate the command with the act and the praise. It doesn't matter how she got into the sit position.

6. Keep your tone of voice authoritative, but happy. Tone of voice has a powerful effect on a dog. If he's walking nicely at heel, let him know on no uncertain terms that he is the best darn dog, doing the best darn heel in the universe. You can actually see the effect this has on the dog. Is his tail up high? Does he look proud and happy? Then you're doing it right.

It's fun to watch a good handler and dog work together. The pride the dog feels in pleasing his beloved Alpha is heartwarming. Go to a good class and observe. If you see a good trainer working a dog, or good handler, resist the urge to watch the *dog*. Watch the handler's body language, how she carries herself. A good handler also has an exquisite sense of timing. She delivers corrections exactly like an Alpha, swiftly. No one holds grudges, though. A subordinate trusts the Alpha: the dog knows he deserved the correction.

No matter what specific commands you want to teach your dog, these are some basic guidelines that apply to all training. We're also going to look at some common mistakes we all make.

Overall, one of the biggest traps owners fall into is that they rush the dog. This is always disaster. Try to keep in mind that dogs learn at different rates. Some even have different learning *styles*.

When we say "Never issue a command unless you're in a position to enforce it," we're trying to keep you from rushing the dog. Owners are impatient. They want to see if the dog will do it. They test. It usually fails. If you tell Fluffy to sit from across the room, what if she doesn't sit? Then Fluffy has learned she doesn't really have to obey commands. And you look distinctly un-Alpha, giving orders that are ignored.

Did you think Fluffy didn't *know* this was a test? She recognized the tone of your voice, even the slightest uncertainty. You sound like a weak Alpha. She's allowed to tune you out. Now, if you put a leash on Fluffy and order her to sit, you sound a lot more like an Alpha. But here's another trap. After a few practice sessions, owners develop the habit of *waiting* to see if the dog will obey the command or whether the owner is going to have to do it for her, one more time. . . . Don't wait. Fluffy needs to learn that when you say "Sit," she must sit *at once*. She does not need to learn, "When my owner says 'Sit' I've got pllleeennnty of time to pick the spot I want." In the beginning, you'll have to be poised and ready to plop her into that sit. If she is going to obey, she'll do it immediately. Besides, when you do "Let's see if she does it *this* time," she hears it in your voice. Your attitude must be: Fluffy will sit. Even if it's because you made her do it. She'll learn. She'll learn that she can avoid having you put her in the sit by doing it fast enough on her own. She'll also learn that she can earn your praise by doing the sit. She really doesn't like having you put her in the sit. She does, however, like the praise. Resist the urge to test the dog, to see if it's sinking in. It is.

Have you watched a dog obedience trial? Did you notice the barely perceptible flick of the wrist that got the dogs heeling?

Don't try this at home. Yet. It took practice. We feel silly, giving our dogs commands and elaborate hand signals. But understand that dogs have different styles of learning. We once thought that dogs had poor eyesight. That isn't true. Most dogs have very good eyesight. Many dogs have excellent vision. Some dogs are more attuned to movement and respond better to hand signals. In the beginning, make a big production out of your hand signals and verbal commands. "FLUFFY, HEEEELLLL!" along with a sweeping, exaggerated hand signal. Make a media event out of it. Remember how much dogs love theater. You can't expect the dog to take this seriously if you don't. Make it as easy as possible for the dog to understand what you want her to do.

Owners often get into dialogues with the dogs. "Now, Rover, all I'm asking you to do is sit and stay for a minute, you see, and then later we'll go to the park. . . ." Quit that. It just confuses Rover. During training time, your voice is used only to give commands, give corrections, and give praise, praise, praise. I understand why humans do that. It's a tension reducer. We like to verbalize. But for now, you have to think more like Rover.

Most of all, training your dog requires patience. He isn't going to get it all in one day. *Respect* that. Don't try to rush ahead. Don't keep testing him to see if he has learned it yet. Keep working. Be assured that he will indeed learn it, as long as you keep practicing.

And remember to be Alpha-like. You give a nice, clear, authoritative command. You issue a clean, *exaggerated*, can't-possibly-be-missed hand signal. You *know* the dog will do the command. You're ready to put him where he should be. And you praise, praise, praise.

Some breeds learn faster than others. Some MENSA-level dogs are stubborn and test limits. Don't worry about it. Practice the basic commands and don't constantly monitor how the dog is doing. Some dogs seem to get it suddenly, all in one blinding flash of insight, fifteen weeks after you started. Others sort of inch toward it. What you *should* constantly monitor is how *you're* doing. Be objective. The big question is, Are you making it clear enough to the dog what you want?

Is your praise effusive enough, or could you sweeten it up more? I was recently asked what to do if the dog doesn't seem to care much about praise. The answer? Praise harder. Make an enormous fuss.

THE ABCs

Every dog should know how to walk nicely on a leash, to sit and down-stay, and to come when called. If your dog has behavior problems, the basic commands will give you some tools for refocusing the dog on more desirable behaviors. Behavioral problem solving always requires learning at least some basic commands.

But first, a few words about equipment.

Training Collars

The subject of training collars raises the hackles of many trainers. Lots of them really hate chain collars. The truth is, used properly, a chain collar will not injure your dog. Ideally, a collar correction mimics a scruff-shaking, a correction your dog remembers from Mama Dog. A quick sideways pop and release will do the job. If your dog goes berserk when you work him in the presence of other dogs or humans, you need the extra control a chain collar provides. At least temporarily. I don't like to see dogs in chain collars for more than a few weeks. By then, the owner should have sufficient control over the dog to go back to a buckle collar. Don't become collar dependent.

The biggest problem with chain collars is getting a proper fit. Owners always buy chain collars that are too big. It seems logical: the bigger the collar, the less discomfort to the dog. Yet the reverse is true. If the collar is too long, it doesn't release properly and the poor dog is hung all the time. There should not be more than two and a half inches of slack when the collar is on the dog. That way, when you pop the collar, it will release instantly when the dog gets into position.

Pinch collars incite even more violent reactions in trainers than chain collars. They look dreadful. They have prongs on the inside. Yet the collar is actually less uncomfortable to the dog than the chain collar. And it's quite a lot more effective. You'll get the dog's attention. The collar is designed to give the

dog a pinch when you tug the leash. Again, size is everything.
If the collar is too big, you can actually puncture the dog's neck
when you give it a yank. With oblivious, hardheaded dogs or
aggressive dogs that must be kept under strict control, the pinch
collar works fine. After two weeks or so of diligent obedience
work, you should be able to start weaning your dog off the chain
or pinch collar. No collar is a substitute for good Alpha
leadership.

Other Gadgets and Gizmos

There's an ad running in dog magazines, selling electronic shock
collars. It includes gushing testimonial from a petite lady with
two rottweilers. She insists she could never manage her dogs
without this miracle device. Well, perhaps she should have gotten two shelties instead, then. Little petite ladies most certainly
can manage rottweilers if, and only if, they are willing to invest
the time and effort in training.

Shock collars and other gizmos are bad news. The shock
collar requires truly exquisite timing, which few of us are blessed
with. It's an easy way to commit accidental training. The conditions where such punishments are effective are in controlled
laboratory studies, where every environmental variable can be
controlled. In the real world, the dog is going to associate a
wide variety of variables with the shock. For example, Tippy
bolts out the front door and runs across the street. A car is
coming. You're yelling, "Tippy, COME!" You give her a good
remote control zap. What does Tippy learn? When my owner
calls me, I'll get zapped. Run like the wind. Tippy may also
associate the zap with the presence of the passing car, acquiring
a new phobia. Once learned, these phobias are tough to train
out. Shock training also has a way of creating aggression problems that you'll have to deal with. One training session can
induce myriad phobias. And the whole experience has done
nothing to make the dog respect you.

Shock collars and other gizmos are unnatural. They don't
make sense to the dog. They require better timing than most of
us have. And there is no way to predict what the dog will actually

learn. Rely on your voice, your body language, and your Alpha attitude instead.

The Heel

Oh boy. First day of school and the dogs are fascinated by everything but their owners. All of which is entirely normal.

Teaching the heel without a chain collar is really tough work. It can be done. All the other basic commands can be taught without a chain collar without extraordinary difficulty. So if the chain collar really bothers you, don't use it. If you feel that uncomfortable, the dog is going to read it and use it to his advantage. Trust me. You won't be able to use it effectively if it gives you the creeps.

The important issue is whether you can and will control your dog effectively with or without the chain collar. For everyone's safety, you must be willing and able to control your dog.

The great thing about the heel command is that it makes the dog pay attention to you. There is a trick to it, however. You, of course, give a good, clean hand signal. Your right palm is facing forward at your side; sweep it forward when you give your most authoritative command: "Fluffy, HEEL!" Well, in the beginning, *exaggerate everything*. Make a big production of the hand signal, and the owner's first step. Remember, dogs love theater. The more exaggerated your gestures, the easier it is for the dog to understand.

When the dog wanders away from you, a quick jerk and release of the leash should get his attention along with "NOOOOO! Heel!" the second the dog stops lunging or lagging, PRAISE. The first few times you practice this, don't get carried away with the jerk-and-release stuff. Give the dog a chance to learn what the command is all about before the corrections get really stern. *An important hint:* Every time the dog is walking at your left side, someplace near proper "heel" position, PRAISE, PRAISE, PRAISE. You should sound like a babbling lunatic: "Goooood giiiirrrrl, Fluffy! What a pretty heel, what a good dog, that's right. . . ." Keep drawing the dog into position with your effusive, nonstop praise. If she wanders, a gruff, "NOOOOO! HEEL!" will get her back into line. Fluffy needs to learn that as long as she is walking reasonably nicely at your left side, you'll be gushing with praise. My students are all used to my most common criticism: "IT'S TOO QUIET OUT HERE, HANDLERS!" Meaning, they need to be praising their dogs while the dogs are walking at heel.

If you don't praise but simply rely on the old standby, jerk and release on the leash, the dog will fight you each step of the way. Dogs hate walking at heel. It's boring. They want to sniff. Give them a reason to do it by praising up a storm. Praise when the dog is walking in a way that resembles a heel. She's not going to be perfect at it all in one day. It doesn't come naturally for most dogs. Don't be discouraged if your Siberian husky has trouble learning this command. Remember, you have many years left ahead of you to perfect this one. The important task of the heel command is to teach the dog to pay attention to you. Perfection will come with practice—and the effusive use of praise.

And, handlers, let's be fair to the dogs. No dog should be forced to walk at heel every second he's out of the house. She needs some time to sniff and eliminate. Teach a release command. "Okay!" is a common one. Or say, "Take a break!" and let up on the leash. Let the dog know he has permission to do dog-stuff, like sniff the neighborhood trees. Sniffing is important to dogs; it's like reading the local paper and catching up on the latest gossip. Or you can alternate collars. Take the dog out with the buckle and chain collar on. At goof-off time, hook the leash onto the buckle collar and give the "Okay!"

The good news is, the rest of the commands are way easier.

Sit!

All dogs need to learn to sit. And not only when told as a formal command. Dogs need to learn that the only hope they have of getting anything in life is to be sitting nicely. The younger you start this, the better. Don't ever give a dog anything until he is sitting nicely. He's ready for his supper dish? Fine. Direct him to sit before you place the dish down. Sit or starve, Fido. It makes for a wonderful life. You'll have a dog who sits when he would otherwise be jumping up, pawing, or barking. You want to give Fluffy a new chewy? Great idea. Make her sit first.

The actual command is not difficult. Even puppies catch on quickly. Unlike the heel, sitting is something your dog does naturally. All you have to do is associate it with a command. "Fluffy, SIT!" with a sweeping hand signal that draws her attention upward. Use your right arm in a scooping motion. To place her in the sit, use the collar to tilt her back into a sit position. By raising her front end up and back, the rear end is led down naturally and without force. You can slide your hand gently down her back, to give her the idea. *Never, ever place a dog in a sit by putting pressure on the hips.* Too many trainers do this. It's bad for the dog, especially large breeds who are so prone to joint problems. Use the tilt instead. With puppies and small dogs, use the "butt scoop." Give the command and hand signal, then place your left hand under her little bottom and scoop it into position. At home, if you're feeling like giving Fluffy a treat, hold it up and direct her to sit. She'll be focused on the treat, and when that happens many dogs just naturally fall into a sit position. No, that is not treat-training. It is not unlawful to give your dog a biscuit now and then, at the Alpha's whim. Just be certain she earns it by sitting nicely.

The moment Fluffy's hindquarters hit the ground, PRAISE HER. Don't scold her if she pops up again, she's not on a stay (yet).

The owners of a sweet-tempered but overly exuberant teen-age Labrador tried the sit-for-everything technique. The Lab now sits when he wants his ball to be tossed, rather than jumping up on his owners. The wife used to dread going into the backyard with her infant in her arms, for fear of being mauled. The Lab has learned that if he approaches and goes into a sit, he will get the affection and attention he wants. Everyone is a lot happier now. The dog still has his normal young Lab enthusiasm, but he sits when he wants something.

Stay!

This is one of the Big Three. The stays (sit and down), and the recall are *the most important commands your dog will learn.*

Don't skimp on these. They are the commands that could save your dog's life someday. Your dog must learn to stay put on command.

Start with the dog sitting at your left side. (Most trainers teach you to have the dog sit each time you stop walking with the dog at heel. Another nifty thing to know. Eventually, you'll have the dog do it automatically. That way, if you stop at a curb, the dog will sit, instead of bolting ahead into traffic.)

You'll give the command: "Fluffy, STAY!" Put your left palm directly in front of Fluffy's nose as you give the command. Be sure to give a clear command and hand signal, so the dog doesn't get confused and start to heel. Pivot out directly in front of the dog. Hold her leash up nice and taut, so she cannot possibly get out of position. Keep her there for a few seconds. Then, return to her right side and give the release command: "Fluffy, OKAY!" in your animated, happy voice. Praise her to the skies. Of course she did the stay. What options did she have? But she gets the praise anyway, just as if she'd thought the whole thing up on her own.

An important hint: Make it easy for the dog. Don't step out too far. If she's kind of squirrely, hold on to her collar so she cannot move out of position. Stay out for a few seconds, give your release command, "Okay!" and PRAISE, PRAISE, PRAISE. It does not matter that *you* actually did the entire stay for the dog by holding her in position. If you build in the success, so you spend most of your time praising, rather than correcting, the dog will learn faster, and *will actually enjoy training.*

Too many trainers let the handlers step too far away from the dog, in the beginning, so the owner is constantly correcting. Don't do that to your dog. If she breaks, you do have to correct: "NOOOOO!" Drag her back to where she started and flash her another hand signal. DO NOT REPEAT THE SIT OR STAY COMMAND. If you repeat the commands, the dog learns a new game, called "Chase me and let's start over!" It becomes a power struggle with some dogs. The stay is not officially over until you give the release command. The dog does not have the power to call "Time" and make you start over from the position she selected. You can, however, flash a reminder hand signal now and then; use the same hand signal that traffic cops use when they want you to stop, palm out. Dogs seem to understand it intuitively.

As your dog develops confidence—and she will, because you let her be successful in the beginning—start to increase your distance and time away from the dog. Don't rush. Owners often give the dog too much freedom too soon and end up scolding the dog too much.

Spend a few days holding the dog into the sit-stay before you gradually start increasing your time and distance away from the dog. Give her a chance to really learn the meaning of the command. Eventually you can work with a long leash, twenty to thirty feet. When she's really good, you can practice with fifty feet of clothesline. That way you will still be in control but she'll learn to pay attention to you from a distance.

After a week or so, when Fluffy is holding her stay for ten minutes at a time, find a new practice location. Perhaps the park or local shopping center. Get her accustomed to holding that stay even when lots of interesting things are going on. The more distractions, the better. The dog must learn that no matter what else happens, she must hold that stay.

The Recall

This is absolutely the most important command any dog could ever learn. Coming when called can save your dog's life. The ideal time to teach this command is early puppyhood. Young puppies quite naturally want to stick close to you, so at that age it's an easy trick to master. Teenage dogs, however, generally go deaf at the sound of "Come!"

There is an art to teaching this, and there are three Sacred Commandments:

1. NEVER, EVER PRACTICE THE RECALL OFF LEASH.
2. Never call your dog to you to scold him. If he's in trouble, go get him.
3. The command you use ("Come," "Here," whatever) is SACRED. No one in the household is allowed to use it unless it's done right and ON LEASH. For example, if

your children often call the dog in play, you select a different command as the Sacred Recall Word. If they often say, "Tippy, come here!" you use another word, like "Tippy, NOW!" as your recall command. Choose a Sacred Recall Command word and treat it like your PIN code at the automated teller machine.

The overall agenda is that the dog must learn that when you give the command, it *must be obeyed instantly*. That's why if the kids use a command while playing around, this cannot be confused with the Real Sacred Recall Command. Then, if Tippy decides to ignore the "Tippy, come here!" the kids use, it's not the end of the world. If she ignores the Sacred Recall Command, it is indeed the End of the World.

Start with Tippy in a sit-stay. When you are ready: "Tippy, COME!" In the early stages, crouch down. Crouching is a friendly posture that dogs seem to find irresistible. Open your arms wide. If she's reluctant, gently reel in the leash and take a few steps backwards, appealing to her pursuit drive. Trainers often teach handlers to give a quick jerk on the leash to get her moving. DON'T DO THIS. A jerk correction is unpleasant. You want your dog to have only pleasant associations with the recall. As she is moving toward you, praise her.

An important hint: When your dog reaches you, go berserk with praise. Totally lose it. Be ecstatic. Pet her, get down on the ground and make an enormous fuss over her. YOU CANNOT PRAISE TOO MUCH WHEN THE DOG COMES WHEN CALLED. Play with her for a minute when she arrives. Make a complete fool of yourself. Let her know she did the most wonderful thing any dog could ever do. Because she did.

Many trainers insist that you place the dog in a sit, directly in front of you, at the end of the recall before you praise. Don't fall for that. Not at this stage. Let nothing stand between Tippy's coming to you and enormous praise. Her sitting in front of you will be important if you want her to learn a proper "finish," which looks snazzy but is nowhere near as important right now as teaching the dog to come running each and every time you call her. Later on, you can add the sit. At this stage, we don't care if the dog jumps in the air and twirls, if she barks, whines, or runs in circles. We care desperately that when you call your dog, she instantly comes running. If you make it worth her while, she will.

On graduation day, during Final Exams, what I look for is dogs who not only "come" when called, but they do it at a run, with their tails wagging at warp speed. What that tells me is that the owners Got It. The dog has learned that if there is one absolutely Sure Thing in life it is this: If my owner calls me, and I come, I'll get a BIG REWARD.

Please, please, please never practice this off-leash. Practice with a fifty-foot leash. A three-hundred-foot leash. Anything but off-leash. I say this knowing that all owners do it anyway. They want to "test" the dog. Please don't. Real Life will hurl that Ultimate Final at you soon enough, trust me. The danger of practicing the recall off-leash is that the dog may not obey. All of your good work will be undone. The dog will learn, "Aw, I don't have to come when I'm called."

My Cassius was off-leash once. He bolted off when a gang of local dogs went by. When he was about three acres away, I called him: "Cassius! COME!" He stopped in his tracks. Then he turned and came galloping at me, uphill, full speed. A visiting trainer friend was stunned. So was I, frankly. But for Cash, the allure of the effusive praise he *knew* he would get was more attractive than the prospect of a romp with his new friends. It only took about three years of living with a trainer to get him there. Don't experiment.

Down!

Dogs don't care for this command. It places them in a submissive position. Dominant dogs resist. Very fearful dogs sometimes act up, too; they think they're going to be hurt. This command is most easily taught during early puppyhood, though full-grown dogs can learn it.

Start with the dog sitting nicely at your left side. "Tippy, DOWWWNNNN!" Place your right palm in front of Tippy and lower it, drawing her eyes downward. When she doesn't go down, put your left arm around her, slide her front legs out from under her, and guide her into position with your right arm.

Be generous with your praise. Remember, she doesn't like this.
With large dogs, you may need to use your left arm between
the shoulder blades to get them down. Practice until the dog
goes down on her own, if grudgingly. It's the foundation for the
beloved long down-stay. Teaching the stay when the dog is down
is the same as it was when you mastered the sit-stay.

The long down-stay is so important, it gets special treatment.

The Long Down-Stay

This is the Big Stuff. The most important training tool you can
have. The actual process looks deceptively simple. You have
learned to down your dog. If you are in a group class, you will
learn a down-stay. A "long" down-stay in your group will probably be no more than five minutes. We're talking here about an
hour at a time. No kidding.

In the initial stages, start teaching this in the house, with
minimal distractions. Leash up the dog and place him in a
down-stay. You'll be right there, leash in hand, ready to correct.
Your correction is the same: a good "NOOOOO!" and prompt
return to where he started. Begin with a ten-minute down. Instruct the rest of the household not to disturb the dog. At least
for the first week or so. Let him get it right.

Gradually begin increasing the time you require Fido to stay
down. You have got to practice this at *least* once a day. Keep
the leash on, so the dog has less opportunity to make a mistake.
Be lavish with your praise. Let everyone in the household make
a big fuss over Fido when you release him. He deserves it. In
the beginning, you may have to virtually sit on the dog. Do it.
It's worth it. Many bright dogs have already figured out that
Obedience Time is when you put him through his paces. Your
dog figures, the rest of the time, anything goes. Not anymore.

Job Michael Evans recommends giving the dog little courtesy
hand signals throughout the stay. They work. The dog can forget
what he's doing down there. Remember, you as Alpha give a
verbal command only once. If Fido does not down, you down
him. Evans also emphasizes the usefulness of this command.
During a down-stay of thirty minutes or more, the humans can
actually *do* something. True, but that is not the real purpose

behind it. The humans have twenty-three and a half other hours in the day to do things. We teach this because of the impact it has on the dog/owner bond.

Some dogs, after they've been through this a few times, simply flop over and go to sleep. Jet does this. She's a stubborn, tough dog and her attitude is: Okay, you can make me do this, but I'm going to sleep through the whole thing.

Fair enough. Who cares if she takes a nap? She's down. That's all that matters at the moment. Some submissive dogs will roll over on their backs. Do not correct this. They're showing respect. It does not matter if he lies on his side or his tummy. What matters is that he stays down, in the same place he started. If he flops over on one side to get comfy, don't correct him. He's telling you he's got the picture: The Alpha put me here and there's nothing I can do about it, so I'll get comfortable.

By the second week, insist on fifteen-minute down-stays. When the dog is reliable at fifteen minutes, slowly add distractions. Have someone go to the kitchen for a snack. If you can, train the rest of the human pack how to monitor and correct the dog, if necessary. You just never know when you may need a tight, long down-stay. Many books tell you that having more than one person work the dog confuses him. No, it doesn't. The dog needs to understand that *all* humans outrank him. The dog will still recognize you, the one who trains and handles him, as the True Alpha.

When the dog gets good at it at fifteen minutes, keep adding distractions. Have someone ring the doorbell. Get up and change chairs. Throw him a courtesy hand signal, as a reminder. He must learn that no matter what happens, he holds that down-stay. Twenty-five cats run past the window? Oh well. Too bad. Fido stays put.

After a week or so of successful fifteen-minute down-stays, go for thirty. Add more distractions. When he is airtight at thirty, it's time to do a one-hour down-stay. Just think, a few weeks ago, you thought it was high lunacy to even *suggest* that your dog could stay put for an hour. Once the dog crosses the thirty-minute barrier, an additional thirty is no great stress.

Now you can move out into the Big World. Do some long down-stays outside. Start to vary your locations. If you have coop-

erative friends, take Fido to their homes and down-stay him. If
you don't have friends who will just love this, start hanging
around with your fellow obedience students instead.

If you practice the long down-stay faithfully for thirty days,
I promise a dramatic transformation. Something profound is
going on. Only a very powerful Alpha Wolf could place a subordinate down and keep him there. Your dog will never look at
you in quite the same way. You will win your dog's respect with
really minimal effort. And it requires little of the dog. He can
lie down, do nothing, and earn lots of praise for it. That's a
pretty good deal, don't you think?

Be sure to be effusive with your praise when you release the
dog. Make a huge fuss. Does the dog bounce around after he's
released, tail up high, beaming with pride? That's what you
want.

Students who use this technique usually report that the relationship with the dog has changed. They find it difficult to
describe. "Her whole personality is different, somehow," they
often tell me. The dog is a lot easier to live with. We use the
long down-stay with aggressive dogs, also. It's intensive Alpha-
training. It makes for a controllable dog. Does your dog go berserk when guests arrive? Time for a long down-stay.

The long down-stay can be especially useful in multidog
households. The owner's arrival often triggers a lot of bizarre
behavior in these packs. Do your dogs begin squabbling and
carry on when you get home from work? Down-stay, down-stay,
down-stay. Even if you only down-stay the biggest troublemaker,
you'll calm everyone down. Some dogs seem to feel the need
to reestablish the entire pecking order the moment you arrive.
That's why they act so wild. The long down-stay will reestablish
the pecking order quickly, and in your favor.

If your dog tends to be hyper, the simple act of lying down
will help calm her. Dogs can't lie down and act hyper at the
same time. Thinking like a human, you might question whether
the whole thing can backfire. After all, if the dog is forced to
lie around a lot, isn't he going to be even *more* hyper? What
about all that pent-up energy? Good question. Here's the answer:
For a dog, the long down-stay is actually hard work. It only looks
easy to *us*. For the dog, it requires intense concentration and

focus. He has to restrain his urge to get up and run around. He has to *think* about what he's doing. It is not at all easy for most dogs. Once you've been working with your dog for a while, he'll quit snoozing through the whole thing. A properly educated, respectful dog will keep a sharp eye on his handler. After all, he doesn't know what you may require him to do next, and he won't want to miss a chance to earn your praise. That kind of focus takes tremendous mental energy for a dog. This will come after you have taught your dog basic commands, and you have begun to vary your locations. One minute he may be napping in the living room, and the next minute find himself on a long down-stay. There is a difference, to the dog.

Students are usually surprised to discover that when the dog is released from the stay, he's *tired*. Dogs are essentially physical. You're requiring that he expend a lot of mental energy. He's working hard.

THE SECRET TO CASH'S SUCCESS

When I adopted my Cassius from a shelter, a collective gasp went out among my friends. "Why HIM?" they all wanted to know. "He's so HUGE!" Cash was well over one hundred pounds of German shepherd before his first birthday. "He's so ROWDY!" I preferred to think of Cash as fun. I took him because I know great temperament when I see it.

Cash was badly socialized to other canines. He was rambunctious. Given his size, he could terrorize humans and canines alike. I can't even begin to catalog the number of items Cash stole or destroyed during his rather trying adolescence. I once awakened to the sound of leaves rustling. Cash had somehow dragged a five-foot palm fond into the living room. It took a while. Only after repeated attempts did he figure out it was more efficient to turn the branch sideways.

Another morning, Jet (my former police dog) frantically awakened me by whacking me with a paw. Always the cop, she wanted to report that Cassius had successfully captured and killed my new throw pillow. Its remains were scattered over a third of an acre.

Not everyone appreciates a dog with a sense of humor. Most

dogs do have one. My former beau was not amused with Cash's favorite trick: slurping a mouthful of water and depositing it in Antonio's lap. I had no choice but to place the beau in a more suitable home.

Then there was the time the Impulsive One got his head stuck in the security bars on the door. I considered calling 911, but I was pretty sure even a San Diego firefighter or cop was not going to be willing to stick a hand anywhere near those giant jaws, no matter how much I insisted Cash was harmless.

After a week to settle in, Cash found himself at the Academy of Canine Training, in El Cajon, California. We were in excellent hands. We quickly discovered that Cash was a natural "pleaser" (I'd suspected this all along). He worked well in obedience. We socialized him to other dogs.

At home, I taught Cash the long down-stay. The impact was dramatic. Cash loved the idea of earning praise. The long down-stay wasn't easy for this wild boy, but if he got praise for it, he would do it. It changed our relationship. A few weeks into the down-stay business, and a friend caught Cash gazing up at me: "My God! I think he's fallen in love with you!" It did sort of look that way. Cash was bonding with his Alpha.

Cash became quite the gentleman. All 120 pounds of him. He could be taken anywhere. Visiting someone at her office? No problem for a dog who knows a long down-stay. Cash actually learned to correct himself when he misbehaved. He adored sticks, but we maintained a strict no-sticks policy indoors. Occasionally, in his exuberance, he forgot. He would quickly catch himself and slink out the door, backwards.

Of course it's all pretty funny in retrospect. I could not have asked for a better companion dog. Once he mastered the long down-stay, Cash had a happier life. People no longer avoided coming over. He got to go places. He learned to be unobtrusive when I was busy and to comfort me when I was sad. He could tolerate being cooped up with two other dogs all day, when necessary. I returned home to find everything just as I left it. Miraculous? Absolutely. Training helped. Cash was so totally devastated by a scolding that he learned to avoid getting them. He became polite and respectful to humans. He let me know I was the Alpha in his life all the time. He figured out it was relatively easy to stay on good terms with the Alpha. If things got chaotic and he wasn't sure what else to do, he placed himself on a down-stay. He knew that was a Sure Thing. Cash loved doing down-stays. He was good at it and he took great pride in his accomplishment.

In 1995, I lost Cassius to hemangiosarcoma. He was only four years old. I still cry a lot. Cassius, however, would probably be pleased to know his legacy lives on and helps other dogs and owners. He was proof of the power of a good education and the right kind of dog/owner bond. He became the best friend I could ever have wanted. Certainly I give credit to the excellent trainers and dog writers from whom I have learned so much. But my Cash was truly my very best teacher. I hope that his story will help you have the best possible relationship with your own canine companion.

CRISIS INTERVENTION: SAMANTHA

The veterinarian referred Samantha's owners to me after she seriously bit a neighbor's teenage son. This was Sam's third real bite. The kind that breaks the skin. Three bites? How did this happen?

Sam was a five-year-old shepherdsomething. She seemed to space her bites about two years apart. Normally, in aggression cases I require an eight-week commitment, at the minimum. Sam's owner's were going through a job transfer and could commit only three weeks. Well, we had to do something.

Sam's owners recognized that this was serious stuff and their options were limited. They were not stuck in denial, as is so often the case with owners of aggressive dogs. We scheduled an in-home evaluation. Luckily for Sam, her owners were exceptionally insightful and caring. Sam had always lived in the house, with the family. That was her greatest strength. Had she been strictly a yard dog, there wouldn't have been much to work with. Sam had bonded deeply to her owners, and that's what we had to cash in on.

Sam's owners had taken her to obedience school several years before, so she sort of knew some basic commands. Sam's bites followed a definite pattern—another plus. It seemed that when a visitor arrived, Sam just sort of lost it. She panicked, bit, and ran. We'll talk in more detail about Sam's particular type of aggression in the sections on aggression. For now, we'll focus on the crisis intervention.

With her family, Sam was sweet, docile, and submissive. No one would guess this was a dog who seriously attacked humans. With only three lessons, we dragged out the heavy artillery: the long down-stay. I explained to the owners that this was going to require a leap of faith on their part. They just had to accept that training the dog to lie down and do nothing was going to help with the aggression problem.

Sam took to it. She did her down-stays, watching her owner intently every second. Both spouses were outstanding praisers. They praised Sam effusively when she was released. She glowed with pride. She tolerated my presence because I was, to her, irrelevant. She had other things to do. She was Working.

Sam's owners practiced diligently for one week. The following week, they reported a change in her that they couldn't quite put into words. Most important, she was becoming dependable at it. They had enlisted accomplices to ring the doorbell while she was down-stayed. Of course, she was on leash and completely under her handler's control when visitors arrived. These exceptional owners were not willing to take chances, and Sam will never be given the opportunity to bite again.

The next two weeks focused on making the down-stay as difficult for Sam as possible, adding in distractions. Essentially, Sam learned the down-stay before she actually learned the command "Down." Next she was taken for walks and given surprise downs, at the owner's whim. We wanted her not only to hold an airtight stay but to drop instantly, on command.

Sam came a long way in a short time. Her owners understand that she is nowhere near being completely trustworthy. But she is better than she was before. The arrival of visitors used to cause the dog to flip out. Now she can't because she is too busy down-staying properly. She's a happier dog. She adores her family and appreciates this opportunity to earn so much attention and praise. She is far more controllable. If they continue to work with her, they will have a "panic" down-stay available, should the need arise. Her owners were also considering doing a Pavlovian kind of thing: teaching Sam to down at the sound of the doorbell. Not a bad idea at all. At least they have some tools. Of course, they will seek a private trainer as soon as they move to their new city. And they will continue to work with Sam.

I would have preferred to spend many weeks with this dog and deal with the aggression itself. But sometimes you just have to work with what you've got. In Sam's case, she was blessed with exceptional owners.

OBEDIENCE GOALS

There are a lot of misperceptions about obedience training. Some owners think it's mean to boss the dogs around. They misunderstand dogs. Remember, your dog needs leadership from you, the Alpha in his life. The real purpose of obedience training is to create a happier and *longer* life for the dog. Happier because he has a job, and a way to please his Alpha. A longer life because the dog becomes controllable. A dog reliably trained to a tight down-stay is a lot less likely to run into the street and be hit by a car. A dog who knows how to stay can learn not to bolt out of the gate each time it's opened.

The great thing about training is, once you get the hang of it, you can customize. Maybe you don't take your dog for walks, you play lots of fetch instead. Fine. Teach Fido to sit like a gentleman each time he wants his ball tossed. It's better than being mauled. Or perhaps you have lots of visitors and you are tired of Fluffy tearing around like a maniac when they arrive. Teach her to down when the doorbell rings. The idea is to make life more pleasant for both of you.

Now and then, someone asks me to train a dog to give high fives or do some other trick. They don't understand the point of obedience training. The goal is not to turn the dog into a court jester, to entertain and amuse the humans. That is disrespectful to the dog. The goal is to make the dog a better, happier companion. In *The Art of Raising a Puppy*, the Monks of New Skete talk about a shepherd they placed with disabled owners. The dog has learned to help with household tasks, like the laundry. He puts dishes in the sink. *That's* the highest and best use of a canine education. Being a shepherd, the dog is no doubt thrilled to have an important job.

The owners of Sight and Sound Concepts in San Bernardino, California, have a boxer named Taz. They also have a showroom full of really cool stuff: appliances, stereos, and TVs. Taz works at the showroom, full-time. He can do this because, when customers arrive who are afraid of him, he can be placed on a long down-stay. He's learned what his boundaries are. Customers often return with their children, just to meet Taz. He's sort of a spokesdog for obedience training. His owners take him lots of places, too. Why not? They have an airtight down-stay available. What's wonderful about it is that Taz *loves* to work. He enjoys showing off. He gets to be with the owners he adores. Taz has learned to sit and stay when his owners need to go in and out the front door. He has learned to come on command. He's learned to sit nicely when small children approach him, so he won't frighten them. It's fun to watch Taz and his owner, John Lapi, work. Taz's expressive face beams as he watches his beloved Alpha and waits for his next command. Taz is an interesting, fun dog. He has a lot of personality because he has had so much human interaction. He is one happy dog. His owners are pretty happy, too.

THE SLUMPS

Going into a slump happens a lot in training. The dog will be working sharp for weeks. Then, out of the blue, the owner calls, "Come!" and the dog ambles off in the other direction. This is almost always the result of rushing the dog. In such cases owners will eventually confess that they've been working the dog off-leash, and it's too soon. The dog learned he really doesn't have to take the owner seriously after all.

The cure: Leash up the dog and work right through it. Go back to basics.

The owner of an adorable and smart little Lab puppy asked me if we could teach the dog to stay in the unfenced front yard, off-leash, and have the puppy not run off after other dogs. "Sure," I said. "Of course, it'll take three to four years." I wasn't being sarcastic. Heaven help us all, a LABRADOR puppy off-leash? These dogs are absolutely crazy about other dogs. They adore a good outing. They're sporting dogs, after all. Talk about tempting fate. If the dog in question was a different breed, a sheltie perhaps, we might be able to get the boundary-training done in less time. Sticking close to the handler and awareness of property boundaries are Sheltie trademarks. But Labs jut love to frolic and explore too much for that sort of thing.

What is the deal with this off-leash stuff, anyway? Owners just can't wait to experiment with off-leash work. Why? In most places, it's illegal. In all places, it's dangerous. It only takes one car to kill your dog.

To be blunt, it's an ego thing. It makes us feel powerful and in control. We love the idea of walking around with our obedient dogs leashless. We want to show off. But is it in the *dog's* best interest? Absolutely not. No dog is totally predictable or reliable. Preparing for off-leash work requires many months of diligent practice. Then you work the dog off-leash, *in a fenced area*. Too much trouble? Think of the pounding your ego will take at the emergency vet hospital when you have to confess your dog was off-leash when he got run over.

FAUX PAWS (DON'T LET THIS HAPPEN TO YOU)

We all make mistakes handling our dogs. I do. Relax. I went to dinner at the home of a favorite trainer and was delighted when her dogs acted up. It's reassuring. It sems that there are a few glitches so common, it's worthwhile to let you know about them.

Avoid Accidental Training

Huh? Isn't training a dog hard enough? How can it be done accidentally?

We do it all the time. Keep in mind how much time your dog spends just watching you. As dog trainer Carol Lea Benjamin, author of *Dog Problems*, has said, your dog is the world's foremost authority on *you*. What are you teaching him?

A common scenario goes something like this: You're at home, chatting with friends, and Rover growls. You would prefer it go unnoticed. You want to calm Rover. "Shhhh . . . it's okay,

boy." Maybe accompanied by a pat on the head, to reassure
him all is well. Yikes! Guess what Rover is thinking. "Wow, my
owner likes it when I growl at people. I got patted and praised
for it. I should do this more!" It's a reflex. Our dogs act aggressively, we want to *calm* them. Wrong! If your dog growls at
someone, the last thing you want to do is calm him. You want
to rattle him, but good. It is *not* okay, Rover! This is the time
for a very stern correction. Use your most ferocious Alpha growl.
Glare at him sternly. Rover had better slink off with his ears
pasted to his head looking for a floor to melt into. If not, the
next correction will be even more melodramatic.

No doubt your guests will be horrified. They'll be a lot more
horrified when Rover takes a bite of them.

We all do this because we're embarrassed when our dogs
misbehave. There's no need. You should only feel embarrassed
if your dog has behavior problems and you don't take action to
correct them.

How often have you tried to placate a misbehaving dog,
rather than correct him? "It's okay, boy. Mommy just needs to
pick up your food dish. . . ." Don't feel bad. It wasn't your fault.
You didn't know you were supposed to correct him. You probably thought that growling and snarling at you was something
dogs just *did* when they wanted you to leave their possessions
alone. Now you know better. An Alpha does not tolerate that
sort of disrespect. Neither will you.

Does your dog *demand* things from you? Petting, a game, a
treat, a walk? Does he approach while you are reading or watching TV and paw at you until you stop what you are doing?
Pawing at you, barking, jumping up, and generally causing a
row are not polite. Neither is spilling your drink or knocking
the newspaper out of your hand. Lots of dogs do this. If you
have been giving the dog what he wants, just to restore peace,
guess what? You have trained your dog, inadvertently, to behave
like a complete jerk. My Jet is an expert at this. She paws, she
demands, she even likes to *order* humans about. This relent-
lessness may have been a good trait in a working K9. In a house
pet, it is not acceptable. Jet loves company, especially house
guests. She can practice her dictator skills on new pack members. She knows only too well that if she tries this stuff with her

Alpha, she will be summarily down-stayed. A few down-stays later and she'll be fine. For a while. Then the cycle begins anew and she kicks off a new campaign for the Alpha position.

When I adopted Jet, she had a K9 case of posttraumatic stress disorder. She'd been dumped, twice already. She was withdrawn and wanted nothing to do with her new humans. After all, we'd probably just dump her, too. She spent her time lying down in front of the door. She was baffled that she was expected to sleep indoors. She responded to petting by whimpering and running away. After a few days, she'd still whimper and run, but she'd return to whack me with a paw and present me with a Frisbee. No, she never retrieves it. She invented Frisbee solitaire. She plays with it by herself. But I started to get the picture. For Jet, attention was a call to action. She needed to *do* something.

She got to join Cassius at the Academy of Canine Training in El Cajon. We found her something to do. I enrolled her in the beginner's class, in spite of her previous formal training. As soon as we started working, a light went on in her eyes. She glowed. At last, something to do. She loved it. Of course, she made everything a power struggle. She'd heel just fine, and even do an automatic sit. She sat sideways. It was a start. It was at school that Jet showed me the first glimmer of affection and bonding. We eventually discovered her gentle side. Today, she even jumps in some people's laps for a good petting. That's a behavior I might not tolerate in some dogs, but working with dogs means being flexible. In Jet's case, learning to receive and give affection were part of her formal education.

Because of her exceptional intelligence, Jet is an easy dog to commit accidental training on. This is a dog who was expertly trained to attack humans. We can never lose sight of that. She's a naturally dominant dog. She'd done some real damage in her lifetime. Cutting her any slack is perceived as unconditional surrender. Failure to swiftly correct any sign of aggression is an invitation to anarchy. Any Alpha delusions she gets must be squelched, and quickly.

Fortunately, Jet has a full-time job. She is employed as Watcher of All Things. She takes this very seriously. She goes to school and does obedience demonstrations, where she can really show off. She's learned that she can get all the attention

any dog could ever want by performing her obedience commands flawlessly. Students are stunned when they hear about
Jet's serious problems with aggression. That's the power of the
program! It works. Jet's not attacking anyone these days. She's
too busy working. It never fails. If I take Jet to a class and really
put her through her paces, on the drive home she'll actually
want to cuddle. I work her very hard and she loves me for it.

So be on the lookout for behaviors you may accidentally be
rewarding that should be corrected.

 ACCIDENTAL TRAINING

In your Dog Log, list some unwanted behaviors you now realize you may
have been reinforcing unintentionally.

Example: Cassius is *still* bringing sticks into the house! This morning,
I got really annoyed at him, so I picked up the stick and threw it
outside.
What Cassius accidentally learned: Wow, this is great! If I bring a stick
into the house, my owner will throw it for me and we can play fetch!
I'll do this more often.

 ACADEMIA IN THE REAL WORLD

When you think about your own unique lifestyle and situation, are there
any obedience commands that could be especially useful to you? Is there
anything you would like your dog to learn to do that isn't covered by
the ABCs? Write it all out in your Dog Log.

Remember, once you have taught the ABCs, you can customize your
commands. The ABCs gave you some very powerful tools for educating
your dog.

Example: Thunder and Noël get to go a lot of places with me in the
car. They not only go to classes, they sometimes have to go along

on less exciting outings, like a visit to the car mechanic. It's a well-known fact that most mechanics will charge considerably higher rates if they open the car door and a large German shepherd leaps out. Both dogs had to learn to stay in the car, no matter where we were. So we invented the "Wait" command. It's a less formal version of "Stay." "Wait!" does not require that the dog be in a sit or a down; he is free to remain in whatever position he chooses. It simply means the dog is not to step past the boundary you have identified. The dog can be standing up and still be doing a proper wait. Teach it exactly like the stay, including using the release command and effusive praise. It works well in gates and doorways, also. Praise the dog effusively as you are closing the gate behind you. It helps ease the pain of your departure.

Obedience commands are only as good as they are useful. Feel free to invent your own. One client wanted her dog to bring the mail. She asked the letter carrier to help by giving a piece of mail to the dog. How did she teach the command "Bring"? Piece of cake. If you break it down into its component parts, you'll realize that it's just "Come" with something in your dog's mouth. She leashed up the dog, had the letter carrier give the dog an envelope, called the dog to "Bring!" and reeled him in, praising up a storm, just as she had for the recall. She had to teach the dog "Out!" so he would drop the mail on command. This dog works at my client's business, and his bringing in the mail really impresses her customers.

What creative ways can you think of to use some obedience commands?

CHAPTER SEVEN

The Official Counterterrorism Manual

IDENTIFY THE PROBLEM

What is an aggressive dog? Sometimes the answer is obvious, as when the dog bites someone. It's rare that a dog suddenly and without provocation bites a human. There were probably indicators of an aggression problem long before the dog acted it out. We just don't always know what we're seeing.

At Silver Wolf Academy, we define an aggressive dog broadly. Certainly a dog that bites qualifies for admission. So do dogs who growl, snarl, snap, or nip. A dog does not have to actually bite to be aggressive. If the growling and snarling are allowed to continue, rest assured the dog will eventually bite.

We also consider a dog aggressive who will not obey his owner. Consistent, willful disobedience is a warning. Something is very wrong in the dog/owner relationship. We would much prefer to intervene before the dog has actually bitten.

Keep in mind that after more than ten thousand years of domestication, our dogs have developed strong inhibitions against biting humans. It is extremely deviant behavior for a dog to shed those inhibitions. Owners often underestimate aggression. Many of us have always believed that a dog's growling when you take a toy away is normal canine behavior. It is not. It is a symptom of a serious aggression problem.

CREATING A CANINE TERRORIST

How does a dog become aggressive? Television. No, your dog hasn't been watching too much violence on TV. Television has done a lousy job of promoting spaying and neutering. Can you think of any popular sitcoms in which the "hero" decides not to neuter his dog? (In real life, the decision might represent pathological overidentification with the dog.) How many shows and commercials have you seen where canine reproduction is portrayed as cute? Irresponsible breeding accounts for the alarming rise in canine aggression. Backyard breeding is all too common. How many people do you know who decide to let their dogs have a litter of puppies because they think it's good for the dog? (It isn't.) Or because they just don't care? Dogs with all kinds of personality disorders are breeding randomly. It should be no surprise that the offspring of such pairings are often dogs of poor temperament.

Crime is also to blame. Rising crime causes many people to seek out aggressive dogs in the misguided belief that this will keep them safe. Criminals themselves provide a ready market for genetically inferior dogs. A well-to-do drug dealer certainly needs a good guard dog, after all. Human psychopaths are often attracted to canine psychopaths. Backyard breeders are happy to accommodate.

The proliferation of attack trainers has caused aggression problems also. We'll look at that in the section on deprogramming.

All of the education at Silver Wolf is based on the wolf-pack model. Dogs are domesticated wolves. That's good news. Wolves are wonderful animals. They're the most sociable and loving of creatures. Unfortunately, our admiration for wolves has spawned a new source of terrorists: the breeders of wolf hybrids. As soon as the public began having its consciousness raised about the plight of wolves (and the significant damage to the ecosystem caused by decades of slaughter), people wanted to own one. Check the classified ads and you're bound to see "wolf hybrid puppies" for sale at outrageous prices. The pups may be described as "25 percent Arctic timber wolf" or "75 percent MacKenzie." Who knows? Genetics is more complex than that. If some breeder claims to have bred a domestic dog to a wolf, I'd personally like to know how it was done. Who knows what you've got?

The idea sounded good, in theory. The fantasy was, you could get all the wonderful qualities of the wolf—great intelligence, adaptability, sociability, and beauty—along with the domestic dog's contentment with family life. That was Lois Crisler's goal when she bred her precious wild wolves to dogs. The net result was unmitigated disaster. What Crisler and others sadly discovered was that it just doesn't work that way. Oddly, it seems to be the infusion of the domestic dog's blood that causes the trouble. Wild wolves are afraid of humans (further evidence of their intelligence). Combine that fear with the boldness of a domestic dog and you could have real trouble. A wolf crossed with a German shepherd may not simply shy away from scary people. Also, a wild wolf's natural daily range is between twenty to fifty miles. Imagine how unhappy the animal will be in a backyard. In fact, wolf hybrids are difficult to confine. Hopping the fence and getting hit by a car is the norm. How would you train this hybrid? Remember the difference between wolves and dogs: A dog can quite naturally accept humans as fellow pack members. A wolf cannot. So what interest does the wolf have in pleasing you?

Please understand that wolves are not mean; nor are they vicious. They are extremely loving, affectionate animals. That causes problems, when you consider their size and power. Even an affectionate greeting can get you injured. Also, they're high in prey drive, and not at all clear what is prey and what isn't, in our world.

This whole hybrid business is contrary to nature. In a real wolf pack, usually only the Alpha male and female mate. Other pack members will be prevented from copulating. Often it's the Alpha female who, most indelicately, interrupts these rendezvous. It's not especially polite, but it's ingenious. It ensures that only the fittest, the best and brightest, reproduce. And wild wolves do not naturally mate with dogs.

True lovers of wolves are putting their energy into campaigning to protect wolves' right to live in the wild. They are not sticking them in suburban backyards.

Some wolf fanciers want hybrids because they admire the wolf's beauty so much. That's understandable. Wolves are beautiful. Consider adopting the wolflike Alaskan malamute instead. These dogs so resemble their wolf relatives that they often get to play wolves in movies: the famous "Two Socks" wasn't a wild wolf, he was a malamute. Siberian huskies are also very wolflike in appearance. What's great about these breeds is that you can have the wolf beauty in a domestic pet. Your malamute or husky can accept you as a pack member, and can be trained. Let's not reward the current irresponsible breeding frenzy. Take your business to a reputable malamute or husky breeder instead. Or better yet, to a malamute or husky rescue organization.

ART OVER SCIENCE

Does all this bad-breeding news mean that if you have a dog of questionable heritage, you're doomed? Not at all. That's one of the wonderful things about dogs. Under the worst of circumstances, dogs can still develop into well-adjusted pets. Dogs are amazingly adaptable and hardy creatures, thanks to the wolf qualities they still retain. Some dogs just need more guidance, that's all. A truly "bad" dog is rare. Uneducated, perhaps. But, rarely bad. If I didn't believe that, I would not be voluntarily messing around with other peoples' biting dogs. I'd go get a real job.

ON FREUD

Poor Freud has been discredited in a lot of areas. And while he didn't have the skills to work with aggressive dogs, some of his thinking does apply. Early puppyhood experiences have an impact on who the dog becomes. As with humans, none of it is necessarily set in cement.

Improper early handling and socialization can set up some serious aggression problems. Unscrupulous breeders often keep puppies confined to a kennel until they can get rid of them.

The really despicable breeders actually place puppies in their new homes as early as four or five weeks of age. That always has negative consequences.

The puppy goes through several critical socialization phases. He must be properly socialized if he is to become a stable, well-adjusted dog. Pure profit motive ruins lots of dogs. Breeders who place puppies before they are seven to eight weeks old simply want to make money. Puppies are weaned at four to five weeks. The breeder doesn't want to spend the money on dog food, so she dumps the pups on unsuspecting owners. Some of these reprobates actually lie to the buyers about the puppies' ages. Puppies separated from Mama and littermates this early miss valuable lessons. It's from littermate play that your dog learned to inhibit his aggression. He learned how to gauge his bite, and how to do a play bite that was all in good fun. He learned to get along with his peers. He learned manners from Mama. Handled properly, the pup learns that human contact is a good thing. He goes on to associate the human touch with warmth, affection, and love. He easily bonds to a new owner.

Through early socialization, the puppy also learns not to be afraid of everything in the environment. Reputable breeders understand this. A responsible sheltie breeder kept a litter in a pen in the family room. That was ideal. The puppies were exposed to all manner of comings and goings, vacuums running, doors slamming, and other sights and sounds of Real Life. Even though shyness is a common sheltie fault, these puppies grew up to become bold, confident, friendly dogs. They handle stress beautifully. If a strange sight or sound frightened a puppy in early puppyhood, he needed only to look at Mama Dog. If she showed no concern, he learned the valuable lesson that the world isn't a dangerous place.

Really good breeders take the time to socialize pups actively. They introduce them to strangers. They put them on different floorings. They subject them to some mild stress every day. The truly excellent breeders started with parent dogs of sound, stable temperament. In the sheltie example above, Mama herself was extrafriendly and outgoing. I saw these pups at nine days of age. Mama showed no overprotectiveness or aggression. In fact, she quickly led me to the pen to see her puppies. She sat gazing up at me, beaming with pride. She wanted to show off her beautiful babies. Their father was an accomplished show winner, of sound structure and excellent health. He was most famous, however, for his outgoing, confident temperament. He too, was a great people-lover. He handled the stress of traveling to shows with the dignity of a true champion. That's the way all breedings should be. They seldom are. It's just too darned expensive. Selecting the right parents costs money. Showing them, to confirm the correctness of their structure and temperament, costs a fortune. Proper socialization takes time and hard work.

Puppies who are not properly socialized become fearful dogs. Some become what we call fear biters. Just mention the term to a trainer or vet's assistant and watch the reaction. They're difficult dogs to work with.

A naturally dominant pup who is encouraged to be aggressive will be a dominant, aggressive adult. Many of you adopted your dogs from shelters, which is good. You may, unfortunately, know nothing about your dog's puppyhood nor about the mother's temperament. A puppy learns a lot about how to behave from the mama dog, so it helps to have some history. But with most aggression cases, after an evaluation we can pretty much guess what happened.

DEVELOPING AN ANTITERRORIST STRATEGY

When the FBI discovers terrorism in our midst, they don't all jump out of their chairs to go get the guy, do they? I hope not. They spend time on strategy. They do their homework, gathering intelligence. They formulate a plan. The goal is to achieve maximum results with minimum bloodshed (especially theirs). That's what you're going to do, too. At Silver Wolf, you'd be given a written plan of action. It's a structured approach.

Some basic principles apply to all aggressive dogs. That's what we'll look at here.

SURVEILLANCE REPORT: The Terrorist

Surveillance must be carried out for a minimum of two weeks. Your report must include:

- Every incident of aggression, including growling, snarling, snapping, and biting.
- Date, time, and location.
- Names of all victims and witnesses.
- Detailed account of all events leading up to the aggressive incident.
- Detailed account of exactly what the dog *did*; e.g., growled and snapped at child.
- Counterterrorist maneuvers employed by you: What did you do to stop the aggressive behavior? How effective was it?

After two weeks, you should have lots to work with. You're looking for patterns. Going through your notes, what do you see? Is the aggression peculiar to any one location? Time of day? How about the presence of other humans or animals?

Or is it simpler than you had first thought? For example, your dog may growl and snap each time you try to place him in a down, no matter where you practice. The only other time he growls at you is when you take a chewy away from him. This sounds like simple dominance aggression; obedience work and Really Tough Love should be your salvation.

If you collect two weeks' worth of data and don't find any patterns, do another two weeks. The patterns are in there; don't be discouraged. The patterns will give you the triggers, i.e., the cues that set the dog off. Once you've got the cues, you can gain control over the behavior. If you're really stumped, ask someone else to look through your notes. An outside perspective can be valuable to any good detective.

REALITY CHECK

It's ridiculous to attempt to train aggression out of an intact male dog. *Get him fixed.* His hormones are working against you and the rest of civilized society. Get it done. Stop overidentifying.

Dogs don't mate because they feel physically attracted, affectionate, emotionally attached, or anything else. They mate to reproduce. That's it. There's nothing sentimental or romantic about
it. Get over it. Life in our world for an intact male dog is
wretched. The poor dog spends an inordinate amount of time
in extreme tension and frustration. It's miserable. He picks fights.
He wants to be the only one to reproduce. He seeks every opportunity to run away, in hopes of finding a bitch in heat somewhere, and to complete his mission of killing off all the other
male rivals in the world. All this is getting in the way of his
bonding with you. Heaven help you if he's actually bred once.
He's obsessed with doing it again. Brawling and leg lifting are
his favorite sports. Give the dog a break! He'll still guard the
house and scare burglars away. In fact, an intact male makes a
lousy watchdog. If he picks up the scent of a bitch, he won't care
about you, your home, or your belongings. Unless, of course, the
burglar is another male dog.

It isn't discussed much, but unspayed bitches are no joy to
live with either. That reproductive jealousy is present in females,
too. It leads to brawling. You are reading this because your
dog has aggression problems. Why isn't she spayed? You cannot
seriously consider breeding an aggressive dog. What can you
hope to pass along to future generations? Moreover, if you think
you can protect her while she's in heat, you're kidding yourself:
males have hurled themselves through plate glass. Do you need
the hassles? A spayed female is a far better pet. She can focus
on bonding with you, rather than on reproduction. Hormonally
induced mood swings will be eliminated. And so will the risk
of certain cancers. She does not need to have a litter for her
mental health. Her mental and physical health are at high risk
if she's *not* spayed. If you feel strongly that she needs to indulge
her maternal instincts (she doesn't), volunteer to adopt some
abandoned puppies from your local shelter. There's rarely a
shortage.

And forget the nonsense you've heard about your kids experiencing the "miracle of birth"—take them to the pound to enjoy
the "miracle of euthanasia." If your dog does have a litter, finding dead puppies will do no psychological good to your children,
and it happens often with novice breeders. Really awful things

can happen to the bitch and the puppies. Get a good book or video to help teach your children about reproduction. Use your parenting skills to teach responsible pet ownership. Your kids will probably miss the entire ordeal anyway, as all puppies are born at three A.M. Leave breeding to the serious professionals.

THE BASICS

The program for rehabilitating your canine terrorist is going to take longer than the regular programs for dogs who behavior is merely obnoxious. There are two reasons for this: First, we cannot even begin to work seriously on the aggression until the dog has been obedience-trained. Second, we must work more slowly with aggressive dogs.

Recall that basic obedience training creates the right kind of relationship between you and your dog. You become the Alpha figure. The dog learns to respect you. He becomes easier to control. The dog also develops confidence as he learns to please you and get attention for positive behaviors. The importance of this cannot be overstated with aggressive dogs. The dog needs to learn how to get lots of praise and attention for doing things other than growling, snarling, and biting.

Fear biters especially benefit from obedience training. All dogs need to go to school. Fearful dogs need the socialization that the group setting provides.

So initially your program will be a lot of basic stay, come, down, and heel. You're not training for obedience competition, you're struggling to save your companion's life That's why, at Silver Wolf, we don't get too caught up in fretting over whether your left foot is where it should be. We fret a lot about whether the dog is paying attention to you. And whether he's enjoying his training. If you find you really enjoy obedience work and want to go on to formal competition, we're all for it. You'll have lots of time to perfect your technique. For now, the priority is to bring your potentially dangerous dog under your control.

The one place we do not compromise, however, is the long down-stay. Our heartfelt gratitude goes to Job Michael Evans for sharing the importance of this with us. By "long" we mean an hour at a time. Any student who fails to practice a long down-stay daily can continue to live with an out-of-control canine terrorist. No one gets out of the Aggressive Dog Program without mastering a long down-stay. We cannot allow it. The entire community will suffer. You've learned how to down your dog. As mentioned earlier, Evans recommends flashing extra courtesy hand signals, without repeating the verbal command. It helps. A dog can forget what he's doing down there. You know how to correct the dog if he breaks: your best Alpha growl, "NOOOOO!" and instant return to where he should have been. If you've been practicing with any degree of regularity, you know what your dog looks like when he is completely dazzled by you. You've begun to look like one powerful Alpha. He'll already be reconsidering whether growling at you is such a good idea after all. Remember, the long down-stay is a *daily* event. It does not matter what else is going on. Tidal waves, hurricanes, earthquakes—too bad. The dog does the down-stay. Every single day. For no less than thirty days.

After a while, you'll notice the dog anticipates the down-stay. Many dogs begin to accept it as part of living with a major league Alpha, and they flop down for a nap as soon as you give the "down" command. That's okay. We don't object to the dog snoozing through the whole thing. We only object to his disobeying you. Once he's had enough education, he'll keep a sharper eye on you. He won't be willing to miss another command and chance to earn some praise.

You might notice that your dog curls up for a nap right after a class or lesson. This tells you something important: you have given the dog something to think about. When a dog has been mentally stimulated, he often needs a nap to get his bearings back. This is different from a dog who sleeps all day because he's bored and can't think of a good reason to live. The dog needs to reorient himself. Mentally, he's tired. The long down-stay requires a great deal of mental, rather than physical, energy for the dog. He is learning and it's changing his view of the world—changing the way he perceives you in particular. This is a very good thing indeed.

For an aggressive dog, obedience lessons give him something to focus on, other than planning his next assault. The long down-stay is powerful with any dog, but more so with terrorists. Why?

It's a theory borrowed from human psychology. You are em-
ploying competing, incompatible behaviors. While your dog is
forced to lie down, and stay put, at your command, the dog
simply cannot act up. The act of lying down is not consistent
with the behaviors that go with aggression. Dogs don't attack
when they're lying down. They're in no position to make aggressive moves on other pack members. For hyper dogs, which many
terrorists are, the act of lying down has a calming effect. You
cannot act hyper and lie down at the same time. The dog is
using up an incredible amount of energy, holding that down-
stay. The long down-stay is your most elite antiterrorist weapon.
Once your dog is completely proofed—that is, 100 percent reliable—you have an incredible stealth weapon at your disposal.
Fido likes to growl at house guests? He goes down when guests
arrive. Fido is harassing the cat? He goes down. Fido is running
around, acting like a jerk? Guess what?

The down-stay is not a punishment. Getting your dog to understand this takes work. What you must do is work obedience
into your daily life. The dog needs to have down-stays, sit-stays,
and any other command the Alpha feels like issuing, hurled at
him throughout the day. If you only down-stay the dog once a
day, in the evening, he won't get the picture. It's easier than it
sounds. When you're doing the dishes, put Fido on a sit-stay for
a few minutes. Talking on the phone? Get him down and stayed
for a while. This must be done in addition to your daily practice
sessions. Your practice sessions should be kept short, no longer
than ten minutes. The dog can't be allowed to get the idea that
this obedience stuff only applies during training sessions. Dogs
are opportunistic. They figure this stuff out. The dog must learn
that you, the Alpha, can give him commands anytime, anywhere.
Until that is firmly established, the aggression won't diminish.

You are entitled to recruit reinforcements. Every adult in the
household should be giving Fido some commands. He needs to
get it through his head that *all* humans outrank him. The down-
stay is something that can happen at any moment. Alphas get
to do that sort of thing. You have practiced it so much, he knows
it could happen anytime. He will learn that his attempts at
ruling the pack will meet with a down-stay. Your task is to remain businesslike about the whole thing, especially in the begin-

ning. Dominant dogs, who are often terrorists, resent being placed in a down. It's a submissive posture. Fearful terrorists don't like it either. They think you're going to hurt them. Many dogs think being downed is an excellent time to snap. Don't freak out over this. Scold the dog, and enforce the down. The dog will figure it out. Owners of aggressive dogs are always getting mad at me for insisting that the dog has a problem. They don't see it, and they don't want to. When we start the down-stay business, reality hits. The dominant dog mouths the owner's hands, resisting the down. The fearful dogs starts growling seriously. There's no turning back now.

The down-stay will become your most elite weapon only after you have completely trained the dog to it. There can be no doubt in the dog's mind that he must go down, instantly. Never forget to be enthusiastic with your praise when you release the dog. Again, you're using incompatible behaviors. The dog will be elated at receiving all that praise from you. His pride in his achievement and total happiness at pleasing the Alpha are not compatible with terrorism. He cannot be happy and cranky at the same time. The reason your dog can learn at all is that he wants the good feeling he gets from your effusive praise. It's something he will not be anxious to give up.

The mistake that too many students make is moving too fast. You simply cannot use the down-stay to counter aggression until it has become second nature to the dog. If he has to stop and think about it, he's not ready. It should look like a reflex. You give the signal, he drops. No questions asked. It takes time, repetition, and dedication. Plan on no less than four to six weeks of intense daily practice. It's more than worth it. You will have a controllable dog. He may still feel like behaving aggressively, but he won't be able to act on it because he is busy down-staying.

There's another benefit that is even more important. Preventing aggression by down-staying the dog avoids the use of strong corrections after the aggression has occurred. By the time we're done with you, you'll be an expert at reading your dog's body language. You will know the "hard eye" when you see it; you'll know when your dog is getting ready to start *thinking* about growling and you will down him instantly. It's better and safer than administering a correction after the fact. You're dealing with a dog who has no reservations about biting you, if he feels the need. A strong correction will increase his aggression. This is especially true in the beginning. All this is new to you. Maybe you're afraid of the dog. If not, you should be.

No matter how much acting talent you have, you're going to telegraph your uncertainty to the dog. He'll use it against you, trust me. It is far better to gain control of the dog before he has escalated.

What will happen is that, in the dog's mind, very slowly, he will begin to associate his urge to behave aggressively with dropping and staying. It's a very delicate connection to make and it takes lots of time. You're basically manipulating the dog's subconscious. This is why you must be absolutely consistent. It's also why you must spend so much time learning your dog's body language. It can be done.

There is nothing more rewarding than seeing your dog catch on. It will happen one day. The dog will be about to pounce on the cat over a toy or something, and he'll stop and look up at you with the most questioning look. YOU'RE THERE! HE GETS IT! He is telling you, loud and clear: If I do what I want, I'm gonna get down-stayed, aren't I? Praise him to the skies. *Anytime a dog stops and consciously corrects himself, you should be thrilled.* It's working! This is the time to reward him with a happy play session and plenty of attention. You should be beside yourself with glee. The poor pup doesn't realize he just may have saved his own life.

IDENTIFYING TERRORIST TYPES

Just like the FBI, you will discover that there is more than one kind of terrorist in our midst. Learning which type you have to deal with is worth the effort. It's the first stage in learning to read your dog's body language and intervene before he gets to act it out. There are different antiterrorist strategies for different types of aggression.

Dominance Aggression

This type should be familiar to you. The dominant dog is our Alpha Wanna-be. Such dogs do not do as they're told. They ignore commands. They don't come when they're called. They growl when you take their toys away. Too many owners think this is normal behavior. It's not! I have two German shepherds. My Jet defines the term "dominant temperament." I can, anytime I feel the urge, remove any item—including a top sirloin—from their mouths without getting so much as a dirty look. The dog has no right to growl, snarl, or otherwise complain about it. It's the way it is. Believe it or not, *that* is normal. They were not always so accommodating.

Dominant dogs are cocky. They are confident. They have plenty of self-esteem. Somewhere, they have gotten it into their heads that they are the Alphas of the Universe. Your goal is to bring that dominance under control *without destroying the dog's self-confidence.* You do not want a demoralized dog. You want a happy, confident dog who accepts your Alpha status without challenge. It's an art.

Dominant dogs aren't really impossible. Dominant dogs are not crazy dogs. They tend to be fairly predictable. Please do not underestimate a dominant dog. They can and do attack. You just have some definite strengths to work with when you rehabilitate one of these dogs. Some dogs are born with this kind of temperament. The breeds we consider good guard dogs are prone to this: if a puppy is allowed or encouraged to dominate, he'll be a real challenge as an adult. No tug-of-war games with these guys!

The dominant-aggressive dog has pretty obvious body language. In fact, a lot of posturing is part of the syndrome. Remember, in wolfdom the Alpha maintains order and administers discipline with lots of posturing and signaling. This is what your dog is doing if he's a dominant kind of dog. Trouble is, he really believes he's the Alpha and has a right to control *you* with his ferocity. Dominant dogs stand up straight; their ears are up, even forward. They look cocky. They look like little hoodlums. Dominant dogs generally serve you with plenty of notice before they attack; they all but scream it at you when they're ready.

They pull themselves up, as if they're trying to look bigger. (They are.) They're sort of on tiptoe. And watch that tail! You're looking for a tail held high, a sign of a dog who considers himself high-ranking. If you see a slow, side-to-side wag, he's announcing loud and clear that he's the boss, and ready to challenge any disbelievers. The dog's gait changes. It gets very stiff. Once you see it, you'll remember it.

People always think there's no danger if the dog's tail is wagging. Don't fall for this. Dogs attack with wagging tails. That high, slow wag is bad news. If you want to know what the dog is up to, watch his mouth. Are his lips pulled back? He's revving up. If the intended victim is another dog, watch for a paw on the back. In dogdom, this is a rude gesture. It's the canine equivalent of the school bully shoving you aside in the hallway. He's looking for a brawl.

You'll note that all this is very stereotyped. It's a ritual. Dogs, like wolves, love rituals. All of the posturing is absolutely essential. It's also your hope of correcting it. *You must learn to read the dog.* That stiff-legged gait—or a "hard eye"—would be my cue to take action. The dog will know exactly what he's being corrected for. He knows what he's doing. If your dog approaches new people with that dominant swagger, he needs a good downstay. If your dog encounters another dominant dog or one who might be physically up to such a challenge, the posturing can go on for quite a while. If the intended victim is one of your own dogs, he may have the good sense to call it quits. The dominant dog is really seeking to prove himself. If the other dog is willing to humor him, a fight can be averted. This is what usually happens in multidog households. The dogs work out their own pecking order this way. The more submissive dog will give in, signal his subordinate rank, and the bully backs off. Most of the time.

Pay attention to your dog's body language. You have a narrow window of opportunity to intervene and correct. That's the good news about dominant dogs. You can learn the art of precise timing. The bad news is, once the attack is in full swing, it's about as irreversible as a high-tech missile being launched at a designated target.

Once the dog has launched himself, he will be impervious

to yelling, screaming, and physical pain. Whacking him will do no good whatsoever. If you are not the attackee and you really annoy him, you will probably get bitten. With some dogs, the aggression can become diffuse at some point. The dog will no longer care about the object of his aggression. He'll tear at anything that comes his way. Dogs who show that kind of displacement aggression are really dangerous. They're not living up to the rules of the Pack Code. Since the dominant dog is seeking to establish dominance, a show of submission by the victim should halt the attack. Often, it does. A show of submission means ears back, head low, tail tucked. Or rolling over and exposing the tummy. In other words, it's the inverse of the dominant posture. The victim tries to look *smaller*. There are strong social inhibitions that keep the dominant animal from continuing the attack. He should be appeased. Unfortunately, it doesn't always work that way.

What can make it all go haywire is the effect of the prey-drive factor. Many dominant dogs are also high in prey drive. They go into a frenzy if the victim starts to act like prey and attempts to flee in a panic. A high-prey-drive dog is turned on by that fear response. A lot of the worst ripping and tearing is going to result from the victim's panic. An attempt to flee is a signal to escalate the attack. It triggers a primitive drive.

If your dominant dog is high in prey drive, this primitive drive kicks in during an attack. A simple show of submission by the victim is one thing. An attempt to run just trips that wire in the aggressor's mind and sets off the chase and attack.

This is why children are far more often the victims of a serious attack than adults. From the dog's perspective they look and behave like prey. They're smaller, they run, they wriggle, they scream. If the victim manages to get away, the dog is going to pounce again, with more ferocity. If it's prey-driven aggression, understand that the dog has every intention of killing the victim. He's going for the throat, quite literally. If, on the other hand, it's pure dominance, you're more likely to see the dominant dog pinning the subordinate down for a few moments. Then he'll back off. He got what he wanted. He proved himself. Both parties can go on about their business.

These dominant guys with high nondiscriminating prey drive

are really scary. They're dangerous. They're actually psychotic. Somehow they lose contact with reality when the attack is in progress. If you think you own one of these terrorists, find a good trainer immediately. Get an evaluation. And understand that with a lot of hard work, you may be able to make the dog more controllable, but you cannot lower the dog's prey drive. The urges will still be there. Your goal will be to teach the dog to inhibit acting on the drive. You have a dog that cannot ever be allowed off-leash. Constant vigilance will be a way of life for you. And you must become one extraordinary Alpha. The dog must become totally, absolutely submissive to you. Don't give this dog too much freedom. He must learn that you have the final word on everything. Only you can decide if it's worth the effort.

Sane dominant dogs, on the other hand, respond well to training. These are the dogs who started by growling at you when they wanted you to leave them alone. Or when you tried to down them. Often the problem starts when such dogs reach adolescence. They test limits. They signal that they're willing to enforce their wishes with violence, if need be. They can do some real damage. But they're workable. A dominant dog can tolerate a strong correction without crumpling. They understand pack hierarchies and respect the Pack Code. They do respond to a strong Alpha. They admire a strong Alpha. Many of these dogs are quite workable, once in the right kind of home.

The best cure for dominance is, naturally, prevention. Proper early handling could have avoided a lot of trouble. They've been allowed to go too far, which makes the owners' work much harder.

What's good about dominant dogs is that they're basically show-offs. Their body language demands to be noticed: Hey, look at me, I'm the baddest dog in town! Often they're very bright. Use this to your advantage! Work *with*, not against, the dog's basic nature. The dog wants attention? Fine. Assemble the household members and let him dazzle them with his breath-taking obedience skills. He wants more attention? Give it to him. Every single time he follows a command, make him the center of attention. Let him be a hotshot for being the most clever, talented, brilliant down-stayer on the planet. These dogs do very well in obedience classes with a knowledgeable trainer. Take him through the advanced class. You'll accomplish two things: First, you will increase your ability to control this gangster by constantly reasserting your Alpha status. Second, the dog will be getting a lot of needs—like his need for attention—met in positive ways. You'll see.

 SUBORDINATE BEHAVIORS

For the next three days, make a list of all the subordinate behaviors your dog has observed in you. For example:

- Last night, we fed Fluffy before we sat down to dinner.
- This morning, Fluffy pushed past me as we were going out the front door to get the mail.
- This afternoon, I shared leftover pizza with Fluffy.

Uh-oh. Fluffy is well on her way to Alpha delusions. Feeding her first clearly signals her higher rank. Allowing her to go through the doorway first also reinforces her belief in her supremacy. Subordinates never get to be first for anything.

The Alpha never shares a meal with a subordinate. The subordinate's responsibility is to wait and accept what is left over. Pizza is bad for Fluffy's health anyway.

How many subordinate behaviors did your dog catch you doing? What do you think she makes of it?

Prey Drive

Sadie killed a cat. Her owner was stunned and heartbroken. How could her sweet, affectionate dog do such a thing? Sadie was a stunning Siberian husky. Like most huskies, she was gentle and good-natured and loved nothing more than a good romp. Never had she shown any signs of aggression.

Sadie's problem was her high prey drive, rather than genuine aggression. She was not driven by dominance or fear, but by her deeply programmed instinct to capture and kill prey. All dogs have some prey drive; it's always a question of degree. It comes directly from their wolf ancestors. You can see it each time your dog goes after a ball. Some dogs lose interest in the ball once it quits moving; we see this often in the herding breeds. The retrievers, however, never seem to lose interest in a toy. Again, genetics is at work. For a hunting dog, just catching the prey is not enough, he's got to carry it around and deliver it. Prey drive really complicates the aggression picture. A dominance attack can be escalated into true tragedy when prey drive kicks in. It can baffle owners of dogs like Sadie.

We can understand this drive by going back to the source. In the wild, an average wolf pack is usually about six animals. What happens when they locate a large herd of caribou? Actually, not much. The herd isn't afraid of a few little wolves. Large and imposing, the caribou hold their ground. So the wolf pack will test the herd a few times. Nine times out of ten, the wolves go home hungry and defeated. Occasionally, something unusual will happen. One member of the herd will take off running. The wolf pack will go off in hot pursuit of the lone animal. The unfortunate caribou just signaled to the pack that it felt vulnerable. This is the origin of the prey drive. Normally, large ungulates don't bolt away from the herd when confronted by a pack of wolves; there's safety in numbers. When one animal flees, it seals its fate. Often the animals who panic and run are defective; old, sick, or orphaned animals get picked off, and this actually benefits the herd.

When Sadie saw that cat run through the yard, the wolf in her came out. In Sadie's head, the cat was prey. In some dogs, the prey drive is so high that even the family kitty is fair game. Sadie's breed is extremely high in prey drive, so what happened was not hard to understand, nor was it an indication of bad temperament. Traditionally, working huskies had to find their own food during the nonworking summer months. The dogs that were not high in prey drive and were not good hunters did not survive to reproduce. Hence Sadie's urge to capture prey.

How do you know if your dog is high in prey drive rather than being an aggressive dog? *Motion.* Predatory behavior is triggered by movement. The same animal or human that the dog can easily ignore most of the time can incite a wild chase by running.

Does your dog take off after other dogs when they're in motion? Or little dogs? Or small children? You may have a dog with high prey drive, rather than true aggression. The breed really counts. If you adopted a cocker spaniel, don't be too shocked when she goes after birds with great passion. It's what she does. Understand that the dog has every intention of killing the prey if it captures it. Although prey drive is not true aggression, it can be extremely dangerous. What if the cat in Sadie's yard had been a toddler? Small children can easily be perceived as prey. A crying infant can be mistaken for wounded prey, with disastrous results. It is always wise to provide adult supervision when kids and dogs get together. With high-prey-drive dogs, adult supervision is absolutely essential. This is another reason why early socialization is so important. Puppies must be exposed to children and other small critters if they are to develop the ability to discriminate.

What can Sadie's owner do? As always, some good obedience work is in order. Teaching Sadie a long down-stay will help. Start socializing the dog to cats. But take nothing for granted with this dog. She may never become trustworthy around small animals, although obedience training will give her owner more control. The owner can give Sadie some safe outlets for her prey drive, playing lots of fetch. You cannot lower the dog's drive. What you must do is teach the dog to inhibit her natural responses.

Puppies of high-prey-drive breeds must be well socialized to children. They absolutely must learn that these are baby humans and not potential prey. They need repeated exposure to little ones, early in their puppyhood. That's the only way the dog will develop the ability to discriminate.

Not all high-prey-drive dogs are killers. Some, particularly the herding breeds, are in it only for the chase. Sheepdogs aren't supposed to kill the flock. My Jet and Thunder have an interesting approach to cats. Once when a cat roamed the yard, they gave chase until they closed the distance a little, then turned and went back to where the cat had originally appeared. I've found no literature that explains the drive to Return to the

The Official Counterterrorism Manual

Source. Evidently my shepherds expected more cats. My sheltie will chase whatever moves, but he never pounces. He'll sniff around and walk away. Some breeds were developed to be flock guarders, rather than true herders. The Anatolian shepherd is one of these breeds. Anatolian shepherds won't injure their own flock, but they are fierce when an outsider gets close to their charges. Conversely, the terrier breeds were developed specifically to capture and kill vermin.

How does prey drive differ from true aggression? The net result can be the same: a badly injured human or animal. A prey-driven dog is not trying to assert dominance; her fight drive isn't being tapped. Nor is she acting defensively. The dog is not feeling stressed. Prey drive is a wilder, deeper drive, more closely connected with the survival instinct. Capturing prey means survival in the wild. By comparison, the urge to improve one's social standing, which the dominant dog is trying to do, is a more elegant and sophisticated drive. And fear aggression taps into the flight/fight drives, which are more closely related to true survival. But the prey drive runs very deep. It is, unfortunately, widely misunderstood. Once again we're faced with the inevitable consequences of domesticating a wild animal. Selective breeding over thousands of years has preserved the prey drive in many breeds. It's useful. It's why herding dogs chase sheep and retrievers dive into icy water after a tennis ball.

While prey drive is not genuine aggression, it's actually harder to treat. You've learned that a dominant dog can be brought under control through firm obedience work and restructuring the hierarchy. A fearful dog can be socialized and made more confident. Prey drive does not go away. Maintaining control over a high-prey-drive dog will require a sturdy fence and a leash, along with lots of obedience work. It's a dangerous drive. When evaluating a dog for protection or police work, trainers look for evidence of high prey drive. It's an essential component for an attack dog. Understanding your dog's natural predatory instincts will enable you to maintain necessary control over the dog.

If prey-driven behaviors were better understood, we could reduce the damage done by dog attacks. It would be better if we could rely on owners to control their dogs, but apparently we can't. If you are menaced by a strange dog, keep that prey drive in mind. You must avoid behaving like prey. That means no yelling, screaming, flapping around, and certainly no running. Children are attacked by dogs far more often than adults, and it's because they behave like prey.

Weimaraners aren't necessarily the friendliest of dogs. My neighbor had two, which she thoughtfully allowed to run loose all day. They growled, they snarled, they threatened. I ignored them. No eye contact. And I quietly went on about my business of getting my mail out of the mailbox. They ran home. Why? They were dominant dogs and I was on their turf, as they saw it. The dogs perceived my refusal to make eye contact as an assertion of social superiority, rather than a challenge. It's what a higher-ranking wolf does.

Strange dogs can be very hard to read. They can throw you mixed signals of dominance, fear, and who knows what else. You won't have time to study the body language and sort it all out. Just remember to avoid tripping that prey-drive wire. Don't run! Don't make eye contact, just leave, *slowly*. I would back away from the dog, rather than turn away from her. Most dogs don't really want to bite people. By slowly retreating, you're letting the dominant dog win, and showing the fearful dog that you are not a threat. Most of all, you're behaving in a non-preylike manner.

Territorial Aggression

Dominant dogs get whipped into a frenzy by anyone or anything that invades their turf. Fearful dogs go into a panic. Some dogs are overly possessive of their toys. Territoriality is a normal canine trait, inherited from the wolves. Wolf packs are careful about defining their territory. Intruders are run off pretty convincingly. It's essential for the pack's survival. There is, after all, only so much food to go around. Interestingly, packs often live side by side on their respective territories with no problems. As long as no one crosses the boundaries.

The dog may consider you part of his territory and be aggressive toward anyone who approaches you. This is most pronounced when the dog is on leash. Of course, he had better be on leash. Some owners really like this sort of thing—as if to say, He must really love me, look how protective he is. Nonsense. You might as well be his favorite stick. A properly respectful dog trusts you, as the Alpha, to make your own decisions about strangers. It's part of the Alpha's job. A dog who is aggressive toward humans and other critters who pose no threat to you is a dangerously aggressive dog. My Jet is a classic example of a dominant/territorial dog. She'll fight to the death to guard a fossilized Gummi Bear on the floor. She doesn't eat it. She guards it because it's *there*.

Fear Aggression

All trainers dread working with dogs who show this kind of aggression. Fearful dogs can bite. Timid, shy, withdrawn dogs can attack. They are completely unpredictable. Unlike the dominant dog, who telegraphs his intentions, the fear biter is difficult to read. You may be talking gently to the dog and get badly bitten. The dog isn't crazy. He's badly socialized. He really doesn't know how to read the environment accurately. He can't differentiate between friend and foe with any reliability. He missed something important in early puppyhood. He didn't have enough exposure to a variety of experiences; he can't tell good things from bad things. A normal dog quickly learns to see his leash as a very good thing; it means an outing. A fearful dog may see it as threatening and go berserk.

Most trainers willing to work with aggressive dogs at all realize they'll probably be bitten sometime. And we're pretty sure it'll be a fear biter. We just can't read them very well.

Fear biters have a hit-and-run style. They'll bite and make a run for it. Compare that to the dominant dog, who will hang on until he gets the show of submission he wants.

Can fear biters be helped? Absolutely. But be forewarned: Nothing can make up for the pup's lack of early socialization. Fearful dogs can learn to be nice pets. They aren't going to change into the kind of happy-go-lucky dogs we like to see. It's a genuine shame, but it's not the dog's fault.

These dogs are produced by unscrupulous breeders who keep puppies confined to a kennel until they can sell them. Actively socializing a litter of puppies takes time and energy. Bad breeders don't worry about this. They're out to make money. Good breeders raise the litter in their living rooms. The puppies are exposed to lots of people and activity. They learn that humans are a source of comfort and affection. They learn that a door slamming will not kill them. Good breeders encourage the pups' natural inquisitiveness. And good breeders only breed dogs with excellent temperaments. Then, when the puppies see the mama dog greet visitors with happy enthusiasm, they learn the valuable lesson that humans make good friends. As adults, these dogs don't growl and run under the bed when strangers come to visit.

Fear biters are often dogs who were separated from Mama and littermates too soon. Callous breeders will place puppies as young as four or five weeks. This always has negative consequences for the pups. They need the company of Mom and their brothers and sisters. It's how they learn to get along.

As with any aggressive dog, the fearful dog needs obedience training. Good training can have a salutary effect on the dog's view of the world. He can develop more confidence and be less fearful. This reduces the need to bite in what he mistakenly believes is self-defense.

Fearful dogs need firm but gentle handling. A common mistake is coddling. It is tempting, with a frightened dog, to try and reassure him that all is well: "Oooh, it's okay, boy. No one is going to hurt you"—along with a pat on the head. Unfortunately, the dog thinks he's being praised for acting scared. It is easy to reward a fearful or fearful-aggressive response inadvertently. Your attitude must be businesslike and firm, but not harsh and punitive. It's an art.

A client rescued a pound dog and quickly discovered he was afraid of moving cars. When they went for a walk, he would panic and balk if a car went by. Once she learned not to stop walking to pet and reassure him, she invented her own command. Next time he froze, it was: "Business as usual, Zak!" Perfect! He's learning that his owner doesn't seem fearful when a car goes by. She just keeps walking. Hmmmm. He's beginning to reconsider his position on cars. Maybe they aren't going to hurt him after all.

Fear biters often turn up in breeds we don't consider aggressive, making the behavior all the more baffling to owners. Just remember that *obedience training is the only hope in working with a fear biter.* Obedience training makes any dog better. Any dog will be happier, more alert, and better behaved with obedience work. With a fear biter, it's all you've got. Harsh treatment will make him worse. Take the dog to school. He needs all the socializing he can get. Many former kennel prisoners are well socialized to other canines. Other dogs may have been their only companions. Use this to your advantage. Your scared pooch is going to like school, if only for the chance to be around other dogs. He deserves the chance. It wasn't his fault.

If your dog is growling at humans or other animals, you must learn to distinguish dominance aggression from aggression induced by fear. As always, the body language will tell you what's going on. Remember, our dominant dogs look confident. They stand erect, trying to look bigger. A fearful dog revving up for an attack has an entirely different posture. The dog's head will be lowered and his ears pinned back. It looks exactly like a submissive posture. It's not! The dog's tail may be tucked, it may even be wagging, but he's carrying it low. The dog may be barking, snarling, growling, or any combination thereof. A dominant dog may give a bark or snarl, but don't count on it. The fearful dog is anxious and may bark a lot. You can actually hear the panic in his voice. The dog looks like he's trying to become smaller. Even more confusing, his hackles may be up. His ears may go back and forth. This gives you an idea of how much conflict the dog is experiencing. He's ambivalent. Part of him is preparing to attack while the other part longs to flee. He's agitated and confused. He probably would flee, if he felt he had the choice. With a dominant dog, things run a fairly predictable course once the dog has initiated the contact. The fearful dog is in a complete panic. He is alternating between aggression and fear, and this is what makes him so dangerous. He has no idea how to handle the situation. Sometimes, there is no warning at all.

A sane dominant dog will approach an uncertain situation with an air of confidence. The tail is up; he's keenly observant. He'll approach and check things out. A fearful dog, however, may do just about anything.

Fearful dogs can often benefit from peer relationships. If your frightened one is well socialized to other dogs, finding a friendly playmate can really help. You're looking for a dog with good manners, well socialized to humans. Preferably an older dog with a calm, placid disposition. Young dogs copy their elders. If you find someone with such a dog, it will be worthwhile to let the dogs spend time together. Your dog is going to learn from observing the friendly dog's reactions to his environment.

Two Fearful Dogs

Missy was a pound rescue who turned up in one of my classes. She was a really cute little blue merle–Aussie mix. Missy's owner's stated agenda for taking her to school was for the socialization. Missy really needed it. She was scared of everyone, humans and canines. Missy's owner, like the rest of us, was inadvertently rewarding her for her fears. When Missy backed away from a new person, Mommy would pat her and say, "Awww, it's ok girl, don't be afraid." Of course, what Missy perceived was that she was being praised for backing away. Her owner and I talked about that.

Missy and her owner missed a number of classes. Her owner never listened to anything I said about giving commands, praising, or correcting. I started to wonder what the real agenda was. Then I noticed something interesting. While talking to my students, I watched Missy. After a few moments to settle down, it seemed that Missy's natural curiosity invariably got the better of her. Left to her own devices, Missy would eventually investigate new dogs and people. She would cautiously approach and sniff—entirely normal canine behavior. I watched as Missy approached a very friendly dog in the group. Without a word, Missy's owner tugged on Missy's leash and yanked her away. I saw the owner do this several times before I confronted her. The owner insisted she wasn't aware she was doing that.

Poor Missy. She started out undersocialized but showed pretty normal temperament. She was interested in dogs and humans, just a little unsure about approaching. Proper socialization would have done wonders for Missy. Her owner, however, had some other agenda going. For some reason, she *wanted* Missy to be frightened of everyone. She was actually punishing Missy for being outgoing and sociable—all the while complaining about how difficult it was to socialize her.

If you have a fearful dog, please don't be a Missy-mom. Socialize the heck out of her. Take her places to practice your obedience work—the park, shopping centers, schools, anyplace where you'll encounter people. When your fearful dog approaches a human or canine, PRAISE. Let her know that you approve. Even badly socialized dogs are inquisitive by nature. It's another wolf trait. Every time the dog *doesn't* skitter away from new people, praise her up. It takes practice to get the hang of praising the absence of behavior. If the dog allows someone to pet her, it's worthy of high praise. She'll get the message: My owner likes it when I greet new people.

As you work in obedience, the dog will gain more confidence in herself and in you. Training her in basic commands gives her a sense of security. She learns how to please you. And it teaches her that she has a good Alpha by her side. By educating her, you'll help her figure out that you are a strong, trustworthy Alpha. You won't let strangers kill her. She'll relax.

Let's compare Missy's story to that of Wednesday. Wednesday was another extra-cute Aussie-mix pound puppy. Wednesday's owner Megan was committed to helping her little dog adjust. Megan was a bright, outgoing person, and Wednesday *worshipped* her. Megan didn't coddle the scared little dog. Wednesday was going to learn to walk nicely at heel even if she did it with her tail tucked. She piddled now and then, but Megan just worked her right through it. Megan brought Wednesday right up to the friendliest dogs in the class for a proper sniffing. By the second week of class, we could see the results of Megan's excellent handling. Wednesday was walking nicely at heel, all right. And she did it with her tail held high and her head up, *beaming* at Megan. Megan gave Wednesday lots of effusive praise for approaching new people and the other dogs. She never scolded her for fearful behavior, but she was quick to praise any signs of interest in other creatures.

Wednesday was a star in obedience class. She was willing to do anything to please her beloved Alpha. Megan took Wednesday just about anyplace that allowed dogs. If Wednesday got shaky, Megan worked her. She refocused the dog from her fear to following a command. A dog can't do a sit-stay and panic at the same time. The sit-stay took enough concentration and focus to reground the dog.

Lucky Wednesday! Her owner loved her enough to do what *was* best for her. She built the dog's confidence through obedience work. She socialized her at every opportunity. She rewarded her for appropriate interest in others. Wednesday learned that the world isn't so scary after all. She felt more secure once she learned her basic commands. Obedience training gave her a way to please the owner she loved so much and got her mind off being scared. Everyone in the group pitched in and helped. They all took turns approaching Wednesday, slowly and gently. We do get superior humans in obedience classes. Megan walked Wednesday around and close to the other dogs, to practice her heel, praising the dog each step of the way. Both dog and owner are having a lot more fun together.

So if your dog is fearful, do a check on yourself. Be certain you are not accidentally reinforcing the fearful behavior. Be firm and insistent about obedience, but not harsh and punitive. You'll get the hang of it.

Looking Out for Number One

Rita called about enrolling Robby, her rottweiler, in a group class. She acknowledged that he was an aggressive dog. I agreed to evaluate Robby to see if he could be managed in a group. Rita's interpretation of Robby's behavior was typical. She claimed he was just "overprotective" of her. Hah! Protection, by its definition, requires the presence of a legitimate threat.

Robby was indeed an aggressive rottweiler. He snarled, growled, and lunged at all carbon-based life forms. Rita earnestly believed her dog was acting out of love for her. No, he wasn't. When anyone approached, Robby panicked. He was terrified of everyone outside the family with whom he was raised. He wasn't at all concerned with protecting Rita. He was in it for himself. His aggressive behavior was based entirely on fear. And it was extreme.

Owners too often believe that their fearful dogs are protecting them. A close observation of the body language tells the real story. The dog is frightened. If he felt he could escape, he would. These dogs were not socialized as puppies. Rita had bought Robby from a backyard breeder who boasted about his dogs' "protectiveness." It's a safe bet that the breeder made no effort to socialize the puppies. The parents' temperaments were probably questionable as well.

Some owners actually try to induce this sort of thing. They want a good protection dog, so they avoid introducing the puppy to strangers. This never works. If you hope to develop your puppy into a good protector, *socialize the heck out of her!* Introduce her to everybody, everywhere. It seems counterintuitive, but it makes good dogsense. By relentlessly socializing your pup, you make two good things happen. First, the dog develops *the ability to discriminate*. It's a crucial element in developing a good protection dog. She learns that most humans are good guys. This makes it easy for the dog eventually to spot the human who does not behave in a normal manner. Second, the dog develops *confidence*. After many, many encounters with a variety of humans, she learns that humans are not to be feared, so there is no reason to panic. Self-confidence is the essential quality a protection dog must have. Sure, Robby scared people. But if some drugged-up thug actually tried to harm Rita, you can be certain Robby would cringe, cower, and try to run. He would not hold his ground when she most needed him to. Robby was much too unpredictable and unstable to ever be a reliable protection dog. Properly trained and well-socialized protection dogs are among the most easygoing, calm dogs you could ever hope to meet. They have nothing to prove and they're not driven by fear. A good watchdog is one that can tell the difference between the kid coming by to collect for the newspaper and a criminal lurking in the shrubs.

So what's an owner like Rita to do? Lots of obedience training is mandatory. That will increase her control over the dog and build his self-confidence. She needs to work him in a variety of locations with lots of people around. Robby needs to be desensitized to humans and other dogs. That should help him calm down some. With Rita's good handling and lots of patience,

Robby may learn to be a nice pet. But Rita can't ever rely on him for protection; he's only looking out for himself.

Crazy Dogs

Are there really dogs that can't be helped? Hardly any—but more than there should be. Dogs, just like wolves, are the most gregarious of creatures. Aggression toward humans or other dogs is abnormal. There are dogs who are just plain nuts, but they're really rare. Their pathology usually gets them into trouble early in life.

What causes these dogs? Humans. Reckless breeding is the usual problem. Trauma, such as a head injury or illness, can happen, but generally the owner knows the dog's medical history. Extremely poor handling can cause serious problems, but not total craziness. Reputable breeders do not breed insanity into their lines. A dog who is completely out of touch with reality, who responds inappropriately to most situations, is the product of bad breeding. Dogs are so amazingly adaptable and forgiving that lots of pups who were abused, tortured, and God knows what else turn into stable adults once in the right kind of home. Again, these dogs are rare. You probably don't have one. As Brian Kilcommons, author of *Good Owners, Great Dogs*, has said, an aggressive dog is fine about 90 percent of the time. That's different from total craziness.

Then there is the dog whose aggression is just weird. It comes out of nowhere and follows no pattern. He's fine with the cat one day and tries to kill it the next. That looks like genetic stuff to me.

Intraspecies Terrorism

We mean dogfighters. Serious fighting among dogs is rare. It is not normal behavior. If your dog wants to assault every dog he sees, you have another kind of terrorist. Certainly you must keep him behind a secure fence and never let him off leash. The dog needs to go to school. He needs to be socialized to other canines. Of course, neutering (for either a male or a female) is mandatory.

The urge to brawl can be a signal of dominance or fear. Watch the body language. Breed definitely counts. Belligerence with other dogs is an acceptable trait in some breeds. At one time, dogfighting was actually considered a sport, believe it or not.

Don't blame the dog's wolf heritage, though. In studies of wolves, virtually every researcher who observed packs has commented on the pack's overall *friendliness*. It takes everyone by surprise. Pack members are very emotionally attached to each other. Of course, squabbles do erupt. Generally these are big dominance displays that no one takes seriously. If things get really out of hand, the Alpha will intervene.

Dogs, too, are pack animals. Normally they're happiest with their companions.

Treatment for Dog-Aggressive Terrorists

Treatment for these guys means teaching the dog to inhibit his urge to assault other dogs. If your dog is aggressive toward other canines but *not* toward humans, there is every hope of reeducating him. Often, lack of proper socialization in puppyhood is the root cause. Hit the books again and read up on your breed. Belligerence with other dogs is normal temperament for some breeds. A Dobie who throws the "hard eye" at other dogs isn't really an abnormal Dobie. He can, however, learn to inhibit this natural behavior. It is not acceptable. He needs to learn more appropriate responses. A Shetland sheepdog who is aggressive toward other dogs is much farther from the norm. It's bizarre behavior for the breed.

With many dogs, what you're seeing is a lot of bluffing, rather than true aggression. A young male who barks up a storm when you encounter another dog on a walk may just be putting on a show. He's talking tough because you're right there. Of course, this nonsense needs to stop. You want to prevent it from escalating into genuine aggression. Barking is a lot less serious than snarling and growling. Remember, barks have more than one meaning. Dogs bark when they're anxious. That anxiety can escalate into real aggression if it's allowed to continue. The dog needs limits and education. But keep in mind, barking dogs *do* bite, old wives' tales not withstanding.

So how do you rehabilitate one of these Terminator Wanna-bes? Step one is to obedience-train your dog. It serves a dual purpose. You increase your ability to control him and you have a way of refocusing the dog when he gets hyped up. The sections on obedience commands will get you started.

You'll need an accomplice. Do you have a friend with a calm, well-trained dog? You must find a well-socialized, placid dog, one who won't feed into your dog's provocations. Jet often gets volunteered for this assignment. She's a workaholic. As long as she feels she is on the job, she is oblivious to the rude gestures of other dogs. They can snarl, growl, and hurl gang signs at her and she goes about her business.

Your next task is to figure out what makes your dog go off. Sure you know he goes ballistic when he sees another dog, but just how close does the other dog have to get? Does he start mouthing off from a hundred yards away? Or does the other dog really have to get right into his space before he gets snotty? Once you establish this baseline, you'll know where to start working with your decoy.

For your first session, have your friend walk her dog right outside your dog's zone of danger. For example, if your dog ignores other dogs until they're about twenty feet away, have your friend walk her dog at about twenty-five feet away. Your task is to put your dog through his obedience paces while the other dog ambles around. During subsequent sessions, your friend will bring her dog progressively closer. Of course, *both dogs are on leashes*. Yes, it does make many dogs feistier, but you cannot experiment with your dog. It's too dangerous. You have a responsibility to keep him under absolute control at all times.

Now, when the decoy dog enters the zone of foreseeable danger, keep a sharp eye on your dog. Does he give a "hard eye"? Correct him. "NO STARE!" Once he glances away (in the beginning, you may have to help him with this: turn his little snout away from the target dog) PRAISE HIM. "Gooood no stare!" And *immediately refocus the dog with an obedience command*. When these dogs turn up in my groups, and they often do, I tell the owners to immediately issue a command, I don't care *what* command. We don't care what the rest of the group is working on at that moment. The second the dog revs up, he gets corrected for the aggressive behavior and given a command. Some owners get really good at this. The rest of the group will be on a long down-stay. Tough Guy will start woofing at another dog. "NOOOO! HEEL!" And Tough Guy will be off and moving. Who cares what command the owner picks? The dog is learning a more important lesson.

With dog-aggressive dogs, your task is to correct and refocus, *instantly*. Your dog can't give the evil eye to another dog if he's focused on doing his sit-stay. Dogs have a finite amount of mental energy available to them. Use it all up on the obedience command. It works. If you fail to issue an obedience command, you'll find yourself locked in battle with the dog. You'll be scolding and he'll be rebelling. You'll tell him "NOOOO!" and he'll be thinking, Why the heck not? You'll get nowhere. The scolding isn't enough. He's too agitated to care all that much. Giving the command ups the ante. Now he can not only avoid the correction, but he can earn some effusive praise and attention. You must make that more attractive than the obnoxious gauntlet-throwing behavior.

The hardest part for owners is to get into the habit of praising the dog for ignoring another dog. It does not come naturally until you have practiced it a lot. Each and every time your dog is in the presence of a fellow canine and he *does absolutely nothing*, it's worthy of high praise. He's learning to inhibit that response. It's not easy for the poor guy.

All this presumes that you've had the dog fixed. Haven't you?

DO NOT RUSH THE DOG. That is the biggest mistake owners can make here. Don't be in a hurry to take the dog off-leash to the park, to see if he behaves better. He is dangerous! Some dogs will never be trustworthy off-leash. Accept that. It's safer for all concerned. Once the dog has had several weeks of decoy sessions, take him to the park on a long leash, maybe twenty feet. See how he handles it. By now you have the reflexes of a fighter pilot anyway.

Some dogs get really carried away with their own toughness. If your dog continues to escalate, and you're doing everything right, yank his collar and get his front legs off terra firma. It *disorients* the dog. You're not trying to choke him, only disorient him. He'll be trying to get his bearings back and won't have much interest in fighting. Some trainers go berserk over this. They think it's dreadfully inhumane to "string up" a dog. It's not. With big or dangerous dogs it's a heck of a lot more humane than losing control of them. It's way more humane than having the dog euthanized for aggressive behavior. It's also more humane to the handler. It's pretty hard for the dog to bite you that way. Of course, you're growling up a storm while you're yanking him up. Keep him there for several seconds. He'll be a bit dazed when he lands. Cash in on it. Give him a command immediately. Let him earn some praise. Don't be afraid to use this kind of force to treat aggression. Aggression shortens dogs' lives. You're not hurting him one bit, despite what he may want you to believe. The only damage done is to his dignity. Ignore those overly sentimental trainers who think this is cruel and unusual. Or challenge *them* to work with your dog. See how far they get.

You'll recall that nowhere in this book, at any time, do we advocate hitting a dog. This is no exception. No hitting. Ever. If you're getting too frustrated to work with him, put him in his crate for a nap while you unwind.

If you're really dedicated to helping your dog, try to recruit more than one decoy. Vary the age, sex, and size of the decoy dogs. You may discover that your male only goes ballistic around other males. NEUTER HIM. The younger, the better The longer you wait, the more difficult it will be to reeducate him. You certainly cannot breed a dog with an aggression problem. If the dog is driven by same-sex rivalry, you can be fairly optimistic about rehabilitating him. Some owners are baffled to learn that their male dogs only want to attack *neutered* males. The dog is just confused. The dog probably looks and smells like another male, but to your dog, there's something odd about him. He knows the other dog is not female, so he gets mixed up. He can probably sniff out the lack of male hormone. In true wolf fashion, he suspects a defect. Some dogs perceive themselves as the designated hit dogs. They think a mercy killing is in order. In the wild, that's what happens to defective wolves. It doesn't seem very nice, but it certainly promotes survival and reproduction of only the fittest animals. Please don't get too bent out of shape over this kind of thing. It serves as a reminder that our dogs are not human kids. They are domestic wolves, acting on instinct. What you must do is reeducate your dog. He has to learn that annihilation is not his responsibility.

If your dog is an equal opportunity terrorist, you have more reason to be concerned. It's crazier behavior than same-sex rivalry. A male dog who wants to attack females as well as males is farther off the mainland. It's not natural. You've got more work ahead of you. With these dogs you absolutely must find decoys of both genders.

And don't think intraspecies aggression is just a male thing. Some bitches are really nasty. Once again, *get her spayed.* Rivalry occurs between females, just as it does between males. She wants to be the only one to reproduce. All other females must be eliminated. Any experienced handler will tell you bitch fights can be the worst. Dominant females are tough. Spaying will help with this jealousy-based aggression. She may never be trustworthy anywhere near a bitch in heat or pregnant female. The treatment is the same: Enlist your decoys. Correct and refocus. And, of course, eliminate the hormone-driven stuff by neutering.

Dog-aggressive dogs, as a general rule, have better rehab potential than human-aggressive dogs. Why? Because aggression toward other dogs is so often the result of poor early handling. The dog simply wasn't given enough contact with other dogs. As a result, other canines make him anxious. He acts it out. Such dogs try to bluff their way with a lot of barking and carrying on. They become overly territorial and resentful of all canine intruders. Some dogs panic to the point of genuine danger. Others are full of hot air. You must treat your dog as if he were a potential killer. Why? Because you just don't know how far your dog is willing to go. You cannot experiment.

If the aggression toward other dogs is the result of early deprivation, the aggression was *learned.* The dog learned it because he lacked early experiences that would have taught him that other dogs can be his friends and playmates. What's learned can be unlearned, to some extent. A lot depends on the age of the dog when you start your serious work. Younger is better. But even a fifteen-year-old dog can learn to mind his manners. Always keep in mind, though, that while your dog can learn to inhibit certain behaviors, the *drives* underlying the behaviors will still be there. Neutering and spaying really help because the motivation for the rivalry will usually be lowered. Because the dog still has the same drives, it's crucial that you avoid becoming overly complacent once the dog is working well. Accept that the dog may not become entirely trustworthy, even though he will be a better pet.

Learned aggression is much easier to treat than *genetic* aggression. How do you know which one you've got? Or whether there is a combination of both? Unfortunately, you probably won't be able to tell for sure. This kind of discrimination really requires an expert's evaluation. To generalize, though, we can say that the more diffuse the aggression, the more likely it is to be genetic. The dog who is aggressive toward everyone and everything probably inherited it. If the dog was acquired from a breeder, I'd sure want to have a long chat with her. Breeding aggressive dogs is reprehensible. The breeder ought to pay for your dog's education.

Aggression Toward Humans

Aggression toward humans is more often genetic than learned. The entire ten-thousand-year process of domestication involved selective breeding to eliminate hostility toward humans. It's counter-evolutionary. It's crazier than intraspecies aggression. And it's certainly far more dangerous. What you do about it is up to you. Lots of dogs have been rehabilitated. Are you willing to commit the time and energy?

Other times, we find a case of genuinely *learned* aggression toward humans. The dog had a bad experience. Or a series of them. Or the dog simply was not handled enough as a puppy. It's common in irresponsible breeding operations; the pups are kenneled too much. The incidents may have occurred at a critical stage in his development. Sometimes these dogs are only aggressive toward a particular human or type of human. Maybe your dog only snarls at men, or teenagers, or persons of a specific race. That's probably been learned. You can probably guess what the treatment program will be: exposure to the type of human he dislikes. You'll need decoys again. The routine is the same. Correct the aggression; refocus and heavily reward nonaggressive responses. In undersocialized dogs, we often see fear aggression toward unfamiliar types of humans. A pup who was kenneled too much and owned by a single woman may go berserk around male humans. Or toddlers. Or whatever he missed. That illustrates the value of socializing puppies properly. The more different humans he meets, the better.

If your dog is aggressive to all humans, that means he shows an aggressive response to all who are not pack members. This is the most serious form of canine aggression. The first thing we need to do is define the aggression. What, exactly, does the dog do: bark, growl, snarl, lunge and hit the end of his leash? Under what circumstances does he do this? Is it only behind his own fence, on his own turf? Or does the behavior carry over to any situation? Does he show the same aggression when you're out for a walk? What about on unfamiliar turf? And how close does the human have to get before the dog acts up?

If your dog barks at everyone when he's behind his fence, but is a pussycat when he meets people up close and personal, you don't have a major problem. Your dog is high in territoriality; he's frustrated by the barrier. Restraint and frustration increase any dog's aggressiveness. All dogs have some degree of aggression. The question is one of degree and appropriateness to the situation. My shepherds, for example, go into a terrifying frenzy if another dog approaches their fence. If they're out, you'll see them sniffing and goofing around with the same dog they swore they would murder. These dogs exhibit much less aggression when they're off their own turf. When you take your dog to the park, is he friendly with humans and other dogs? If so, your dog's aggression was territorial. You need a good fence and a leash—there's no good reason to take chances. Avoid taking your dog for walks in your own neighborhood; each time the dog eliminates, he (or she) is marking territory. If allowed to mark up the whole neighborhood, the dog will claim it and start showing the same aggression all over the place. This kind of aggression is just as common in females as in males.

Then there are the dogs who are just as aggressive to people they meet *off* their own turf. If your dog is one of these, you've got a very serious problem. You have decisions to make. The dog will never be trustworthy off-leash. Life with one of these dogs is no fun for either of you.

Your first task is to get back into your Dog Log. Spend at least two weeks recording, in detail, each and every incident of aggression. Include details about the day, time, location, and situation. Describe exactly what your dog did. This is a lot of work, but you must do it if you hope to save your dog. After two weeks' worth of data, go through your notes and look for patterns. What you're looking for are the *triggers* that set the dog off. At the same time, you should be diligently working the dog in obedience.

What you find may amaze you. The aggression may be narrower than it looked. Or the dog may truly be aggressive to all humans, under all circumstances. What can you do then? Get with the vet, find out about treatment options she may be able to offer. Get with the Really Tough Love Program, which is described later in this chapter. Do the desensitization work outlined earlier.

The narrower the aggression, the more likely you are to be able to cure it. For instance, suppose after two weeks of intelligence gathering you find a pattern. Your dog lunges and barks only in the presence of small children. When adults come close, he's calm. Now you've got lots to work with; you must socialize the dog to children. Use the correct and refocus techniques to desensitize him. Of course, *the dog will be on a leash at all times.* Your dog is afraid of small children, so your task will be to teach him that they are not dangerous. Remember, this kind of aggression was learned. With a lot of hard work and diligence, he may be able to unlearn it.

What if your dog is aggressive toward *you* or other household members? Again, do your data gathering. Let's figure out what it all means. When is he aggressive? How does he express it? The dog who growls when you move him off the bed is most likely acting out of dominance. Dominance aggression is often workable. Again, look for the randomness. The more random the violence, the more likely it is fear-based. Fear aggression is always tough to deal with.

Too Little, Too Late: Hank

Hank was a golden retriever with a serious aggression problem. Aggression in that breed is always alarming. Goldens are supposed to be the world's gentlest, best-natured dogs. So when we see aggression in a golden, we have to suspect genetics or a medical cause. Hanks' owner was referred by the vet who had found no physical cause for the dog's behavior.

Hanks' owner Sara was a lovely, gentle lady who dearly wanted to help the dog. She got Hank neutered. She took Hank to school. He was quite unusual in that he was more belligerent off his own turf than he was at home. That suggests fear, rather than dominance. A dominant dog is a tiger at home, but may be less cocky on strange territory. Hank was aggressive with Sara. If she gave him a command he didn't care for, he growled and snapped. Hank was a true problem dog. To complicate the picture, Sara had a nine-year-old daughter. Hank had been okay with the little girl thus far, but Sara was growing concerned. She scheduled an in-home consultation.

With me, Hank was the picture of humility and submission. He greeted me in a belly crawl; he was the Eddie Haskell of dogdom. It's a common problem for trainers: dogs aren't always willing to show us their real stuff, they know an Alpha when they see one.

Sara put Hank on Really Tough Love. Hank's behavior got worse. It happens sometimes that aggression often gets worse before it gets better. The pressure is really on the dog; he's expected to obey commands and work for a living. Some dogs can't handle it. Hank started biting his owner. Sara hung in as long as she could.

Eventually, Sara had Hank euthanized. Their relationship had been irreparably ruptured. She could no longer trust her dog. She had her child to consider. Did she do the right thing? For this particular owner, at this particular time, yes. She took Hank as far as he could go. She was afraid of him. He failed to respond to her loving handling. She did everything she could have done. None of that made it any easier. Sara agonized over her decision. Someday, Sara will get another dog. She's learned so much through her work with Hank that she will be a fabulous handler.

There are millions of deserving dogs that need homes and will be able to receive and return the love that Sara has to offer.

The real culprit in this sad case was not Hank. It was the irresponsible jerks who bred him. This was not the first litter they offered for sale. They're breeding crazy dogs and producing more crazy dogs. They're causing tremendous heartache. They're contributing to the ruination of a wonderful breed. When someone asks my advice about choosing a good family dog, I *should* be able to say, without reservation, "Golden retriever!" Unfortunately, because of people like the ones who bred Hank, I must include a lengthy preamble about finding a reputable breeder and checking on early socialization. What's truly tragic is that Hank was the *third* aggressive golden I encountered in one short summer. Until this breeding plague is brought under control, we'll see more stories like Sara's.

THE CRIMINAL PROFILE

For each incident you recorded in your surveillance report (see page 123), identify the *type* of aggression you believe your dog can be charged with. There may be more than one dynamic at work. For example, if your dog barks, growls, snarls, and tries to break the windows out of your car when he sees another dog go by, he could be driven by strong feelings of territoriality about the car, and he could also be exhibiting fear or dominance aggression. Study the body language to sort it out.

For each incident of aggression you identified, jot some notes about what made it look like that type of aggression.

Example: Cassius met Buttercup, the neighbor's cow, today from the other side of the fence. She was his first cow. Cash was barking up a storm—territorial. His head was low, his ears kept swiveling back and forth, and his hackles were up. He was wagging his tail, but carrying it low—fear! Buttercup scared the daylights out of Cash! The body language was totally consistent with fear aggression. This was Cash's first encounter with an animal larger than himself.

Now, looking over your notes, determine whether or not the aggression was appropriate to the situation. In the example above, Cash's territorial woofing at the fence line is pretty normal dog behavior. Cash's fear aggression response gives us a great deal of insight into his overall temperament and character. We know he will be a high risk in strange situations; his reflex is to panic and he displays aggression when he is frightened. What we can't tell from this evidence is how much of the aggression was caused by barrier frustration.

Is aggression *ever* appropriate? Yes! A client, Sandy, had a collie-mix, three-year-old neutered male dog. The dog was well socialized and friendly to humans and canines. Sandy and her dog lived in a beautiful, peaceful mountain community that was being terrorized by a local drug addict. He eventually showed up in Sandy's vestibule, waving a broken bottle and screaming threats. The collie-mix dog stood in front of the thug, snarling and growling. When the man continued to advance, the dog bit him solidly on the arm. The criminal retreated.

Did the collie-mix dog show aggression? You bet! The dog's aggression was entirely appropriate and protective. Lots of people end up in Sandy's vestibule, friends and neighbors. The dog had the discrimination ability to select only one that needed biting. He issued appropriate warning growls and threats and bit with great confidence when it was necessary. The dog was not protection-trained. His case illustrates what a good dog with excellent temperament and socialization will do, quite naturally, for the family and home he loves. As a guard dog, this little collie-mix is of far more valuable than the thousands of unstable, unreliable, unpredictable, crazy "protection" dogs being churned out by irresponsible breeders.

GATHERING MORE INTELLIGENCE DATA

Your dog has been reliably identified as a true canine terrorist. You know the terrorist organization to which he claims allegiance. Now what? You're almost ready to finalize your operation. Now you *must* get the dog to the vet for a complete checkup. Some aggressive behaviors have physical causes. It would be patently unfair to convict the dog without giving him the opportunity to introduce expert testimony. Your veterinarian may prescribe a course of drug therapy (for the *dog*, not the frazzled owner). You, of course, will follow her recommendations to the letter. Once the vet has ruled out a possible medical problem, you can proceed to the counterterrorism.

THE ANTITERRORISM MANIFESTO: THE REALLY TOUGH LOVE PROGRAM

General Guidelines

In addition to your program of teaching basic commands and desensitizing the dog to whatever stimulates the aggression, you must follow these general guidelines for living with an aggressive dog:

1. Daily obedience lessons, no more than ten minutes at a time. Ideally, two ten-minute sessions each day.
2. The dog is not allowed on the furniture.
3. NO TREATS.
4. Owner engages in Alpha Activities: you go through the doorway first; you order the sleeping dog to "Move" if you need to get by.
5. No outings, other than to school or the vet.
6. No less than one long (thirty minutes or longer) down-stay per day. Down-stays and sit-stays randomly ordered throughout the day, at the Alpha's whim.
7. If the dog is not in the process of obeying a command, he does not exist. The dog must earn every shred of attention he gets.
8. No gratuitous petting. He gets petting only after following a command.
9. The dog sleeps in the house, but not on the bed of any human. Ideally, he sleeps in his crate in the Alpha's room.
10 . Dress Code Strictly Enforced: the dog will wear his buckle collar and leash *at all times*, even in the house.

It's just the beginning. Note that obedience commands are freely given, at the Alpha's discretion. The actual lessons need to be kept short. This prevents boredom for both of you. It also prevents overstimulating an aggressive dog. End each session on a happy note. Go back to a command the dog knows and follows reasonably well. His most recent memory of training should be happy. Reward him with lots of praise and a short play session with you.

Psychological Warfare

Obedience lessons are not limited to your practice sessions. Obedience training is going to become second nature to you. All throughout the day, you will be randomly issuing commands. The dog cannot be allowed to get it into his head that he only needs to obey during practice time. He must also learn that the Alpha is running things. With enough of the right kind of stimulation, the kind that comes from being at the ready for your next instructions, he isn't going to have a lot of spare time on his paws to think about biting and growling. Being alert for commands and obeying the Alpha are going to become the dog's career. The terrorist never knows when you are going to issue a command and insist on instant compliance. You're the stealth trainer.

You will have the dog on a leash, at all times. You must never be in a situation in which you are not in a position to correct the dog, instantly. Whenever that happens, you go back to square one. You must, for the safety of all concerned, never be out of a position to control an aggressive dog. Don't worry, it won't last forever. You'll see.

TOUGH LOVE: YOUR DOG'S PERMANENT RECORD

In your Dog Log, record the date you officially place the dog on Tough Love. Each week, jot some notes about his progress, especially how he's doing in his daily obedience lessons.

Also, record any lapses. Did a well-meaning relative slip him some table scraps? Identify the culprit. Make some notes about the culprit's relationship to the dog. What were the culprit's real motivations?

Common excuses will be lines like "Oh, he was sooo hungry!" Nonsense. The dog gets a premium-quality dog food. He's better nourished than most of us. Or, "Oh, I felt so sorry for him!" Sorry for this dog?

Why? He's got owners who love him so much they're willing to turn their
whole lives topsy turvy to carry out the Really Tough Love Program. He's
the luckiest dog around!

Keep track of your dog's progress on the program. Always keep an
eye out for patterns of problem behaviors and possible triggers. And,
always, always keep track of saboteurs. What are their *real* motivations?

Praise!

Never forget the importance praise has for your dog. With some
dogs, you may have to modulate it. You want to sound animated
and happy, but not histrionic. Overstimulation is a real problem
with many aggressive dogs. A happy tone of voice and a scratch
on the chest will keep her interested and focused at the same
time. With fearful dogs, you must also watch sensory overload.
Chest scratching and a happy "Good dog!" will get your point
across.

Most students readily understand the use of commands.
Praising properly is more difficult to learn. You must train yourself to praise not only a correct response to a command, but
also the absence of bad behaviors. For example, Fluffy starts to
gnaw on a chair leg. You issue an Alpha-style "NOOOOO!"
Fluffy, very impressed, stops gnawing. PRAISE HER. It's difficult
to teach yourself to reward nonbehaviors, but you absolutely
must do it. Your dog throws another dog the "hard eye." Correct
her: "NOOOOO STARE!" She glances away. PRAISE HER
UP! Yes, this is more work for you than for the dog. Eventually
you'll do it out of habit. I wander around all day giving little
"Good Dog!"'s. Dogs notice. They care. They begin to understand exactly what's expected of them. A dog may stop what
she's doing in response to your Alpha growl. For that moment.
That's good, but not good enough. You must make it clear to
the dog that stopping the chewing was precisely what you wanted
her to do and that you are just delighted that she did this fine
thing. You and your dog will come to a very special kind of
understanding this way. She will know not only what she mustn't
do, but what she can do to earn your praise. The truth is, praise

is a more powerful tool than correction. Dogs care more about pleasing you than avoiding a correction. That's one reason we love them so much.

Some training manuals recommend "stimulus substitution": if Fluffy gnaws the table leg, you divert her with a new chewy. What a wonderful place Fluffy's world must be. Life is one giant pet supply store. Fluffy hasn't learned anything. This practice sends the wrong message, and looks too much like bribery. Fluffy is smart enough to learn that putting her mouth on anything but an authorized chewy is bad news. Don't generate confusion by providing too many chewies. It's easier for the dog to distinguish authorized chewies from Everything Else on the Planet if she only has one or two. She's fine. Don't confuse her by offering a replacement chewy. What she'll learn if she is really clever, and most dogs are, is that the shortest route to new rawhide is the chair leg.

So learn your newest commandment: *Every time the dog stops doing the unwanted behavior in response to a correction, praise her.*

For Adults Only

Sorry, there's nothing racy going on. It's just that working an aggressive dog is really an adults-only project. In normal circumstances, school-age children can be wonderful handlers. They understand about rules and lessons. Children cannot be allowed to work with, train or correct an aggressive dog. The current ratio of child to adult bite victims is three to one. There are many possible explanations. Children have a hard time gauging their corrections and may antagonize the dog. Children's body language is different than adults'; their movements are more abrupt. Their voices are higher-pitched and not well modulated. They often behave like prey. It sets some dogs off. Do not put your children at risk. Rehabilitating a canine terrorist is an adult activity. Certainly explain to your children that Rover is having some problems with his behavior and you're trying to help him. Encourage them to be involved in less direct ways. Read this book with them. They will find it fascinating, and their SAT scores will improve. Rent some dog-care videos. Let them understand that the obedience work is very important. If they feel a little left out, it's better than their having to have facial reconstructive surgery.

By diligently working with your dog, you are teaching your children a valuable lesson. You are teaching them that pets are not disposable. Congratulate yourself. You didn't dump the dog off at the pound at the first sign of trouble. You're investing your time, money, and energy in being a superresponsible pet owner. Your children are going to learn a lot about commitment and responsibility from this experience. At the very least, they will know you did everything possible to help your troubled pup. Keep that in mind when frustration sets in.

Corrections

Well, there's certainly nothing more fun than having to administer a strong correction to a dog who wants to bite. Fortunately, when it's done right, it doesn't have to be too often.

Keep in mind that your task has been to reorganize Fido's world so that he has fewer opportunities to misbehave. By now, his daily planner is filled with sit-stays and down-stays and coming when called. He has started to figure out that life can be really pleasant when you are doing the right stuff and getting lots of praise. Wouldn't it be nice if that's all there was to it? With normal dogs, it is. But you have a terrorist in your pack, and at some point he will have to be corrected for specific terrorist acts.

It's not so tough to correct an aggressive dog. All you need are the reflexes and central nervous system of a military test pilot. So, what's an owner to do? What we'll have to do is set up a sting operation. You'll determine what is likely to bring out the aggressive behavior, and then make it happen!

At the same time, you must continue diligently teaching your dog manners and make certain the only thoughts entering his canine brain have to do with perfecting his down-stay.

Scared Straight

With fearful dogs, the emphasis is definitely on rewarding non-fearful, appropriate behaviors. Aggressive behavior must still be corrected, but with a lighter touch. These dogs respond better to motivational training. The dog needs to boost his confidence. Obedience training does that. The world becomes a less scary place for an educated dog. An overly harsh, ill-timed correction convinces these dogs they were right all along and should have started biting sooner.

Again, learn to reward nonbehavior. For example, if Fang normally growls and runs under the chair when a guest arrives, you escort Fang to the door and place him in a sit-stay (he is on a leash, after all). It is not cheating to give him a little courtesy reminder, such as, "Fang, don't even *think* about it." This time, when Fang is nicely sit-staying and does not growl when you open the door, PRAISE HIM UP. Greet people in a happy, friendly manner. Your dog, once he recognizes you as the Alpha wolf, is going to watch your reactions to people. It's the Alpha who gets to decide what to do with intruders who wander onto pack territory. Thus your dog will expect to take his cues from you. He'll take your word for it about new people. When the dog shows a *friendly* interest in a visitor, it's worthy of high praise. No, it will not make him a less efficient watchdog. (Fearful dogs are completely unreliable as guard dogs anyway.) He'll still bark at strange noises. He must learn not to growl at invited guests.

With these dogs, you are basically tugging them gently along in hopes that they will discover the world isn't as scary as they thought.

Instruct visitors to let the dog approach at his own pace. There are far too many self-proclaimed "dog people" who seem to think they have an unassailable right to force themselves on any dog they see. Don't invite them to your home. If the dog is getting shaky, let him spend some time in his crate. He's not going to get over this in one day. It took a lot of early mishandling and neglect to get him to this point. Let him go slowly.

MULTIPLE ASSOCIATIONS

Canine aggression is a challenging problem. What makes it even more difficult is the overlap among categories. Your dog can claim allegiance to more than one terrorist organization. A dominant dog, for example, may also show fear aggression under some circumstances. A fearful dog may be high in prey drive.

A dog who is simply high in dominance and will to power has the best prognosis. Remember, your job is to become more dominant than the dog. Such dogs respond well to training.

Unfortunately, the overwhelming majority of aggression cases we see are fear-based. The challenge is to figure out exactly what is going on in the dog's head. Some fearful dogs will get better with solid obedience work. Their self-confidence will increase. They will respond to socialization; they have enough mental flexibility to change their opinions about what is threatening and what isn't. These are dogs with basically sound temperament.

The Hanks of the world are different. They're badly socialized and had poor early handling, if they had any at all. But they started out with poor genetic material. That's not to say that a dog like Hank could not have been rehabilitated. Anything is possible. If you have a dog like Hank, all you can do is follow the program as diligently as you can. I never stop being amazed at the dogs' capacity to change. This high degree of adaptability is inherited directly from the wolf. Their ability to adapt to their circumstances is truly phenomenal. Week after week, owners enroll in my classes highly skeptical. No way, they insist, will their dogs *ever* pay attention or behave themselves in the presence of other dogs and humans. Within a few weeks, those same dogs are doing their down-stays, oblivious to the rest of the crowd. It's not magic; the dogs simply figured out what was required of them. The owners used praise to make it worthwhile for the dogs. The dogs simply got used to the new environment.

DISPLACEMENT AGGRESSION

Jack was in his car with Rudy, his German shepherd. Rudy spotted a dog walking with his owner and went berserk. He barked, he growled, he pounded the car window with his paws. "Shh, Rudy! Settle down!" Jack commanded as he gave Rudy's collar a tug. Rudy whipped around sharply and bit Jack on the arm.

What was that all about? Rudy demonstrated displacement aggression. The real object of his loathing was the other dog.

When his frustration level got high enough, he displaced his aggression onto the nearest target, his owner. This kind of aggression is really bad news.

A trainer who specializes in security dogs told me recently that this sort of thing is quite common with his dogs! If so, there are two dynamics at work: First, the dog is being overagitated. Second, the dog is not stable enough for civilian protection work. Sorry, but it's true.

When Rudy got agitated, he lost contact with reality. That's one definition of a psychosis. Rudy had no real desire to injure his owner, but his reality-testing ability collapsed under stress. The dog's excitability threshold is too low. A sane, stable dog may still bark up a storm when confronted with another dog while confined. But the sane dog doesn't get agitated to the extent that Rudy did. Rudy certainly needs to be socialized to other dogs and desensitized. He could still be a good companion dog, but Jack has to face the fact that he has an emotionally unstable dog.

Are there really neurotic and psychotic dogs? Absolutely. Keep in mind how much alike humans and canines are emotionally. Dogs experience the same kinds of feeling states that we do. Dogs live much closer to their feelings. They don't intellectualize and distance themselves from their emotions. Some dogs are really good at expressing their feelings. My Cassius is like that; one never has to guess what he's feeling, his face, his ears, and his tail tell all. It's delightful. Maybe dogs can be a good influence on those of us who tend to get out of touch with our own feelings.

So if your dog exhibits this displacement stuff, be especially concerned. Learn to tell when he's getting overagitated, and get him down-stayed immediately. These dogs need grounding; it's the only way they can regain contact with reality. A down-stay really helps. And please don't attempt to train one of these dogs for protection work; they're not cut out for it.

COVERT OPERATIONS: THE HAZARDS

The biggest threat to success in rehabilitating your canine terrorist is not the dog. It's not his age, sex, breed, or temperament.

Your biggest enemy is what psychologists call denial. We have a hard time seeing that our dog has an aggression problem. We don't want to see it. At least healthy, well-adjusted humans don't want to believe their dogs are dangerous. So we rewrite history, make excuses, and generally hope the problem goes away.

The only thing worse than having an aggressive dog is having one who is aggressive toward *you*. The dog is supposed to love you. It hurts when your dog threatens you.

First of all, if your dog growls, snarls, snaps, or generally disobeys you, it does not mean he doesn't love you. Subordinate wolves love each other and bond very deeply. It is not the same quality of love and deep admiration they all feel for the Alpha, however. Don't settle for less. Once you have formed that kind of bond with your pet, you won't be able to settle for less.

The actual process of escalating aggression is fairly predictable. The first time your dog growls at you because he wants you to back off, he is testing you. Unless firmly corrected, he files this lesson away. He has just been trained that he can get his way through aggression. Eventually there will be another confrontation. It's what dogs are genetically programmed to do: lead or be led. As the dog matures, the growling can easily lead to snarling and eventually to biting.

So much of this heartache could be prevented. Little puppies invariably try an experimental growl during puppyhood. Perhaps the little squirt decided she didn't care for being brushed and let you know loud and clear. *That* was the time for a stern correction. Too often, owners fail to take this kind of rebellion seriously.

 DENY WHAT YOU CAN, REPRESS THE REST

Looking at the past, list some incidents of problem aggression that you didn't know you were supposed to take seriously.

Example: Noël had his first experience with a brush at age seven weeks. He didn't care for it, and he let me know this by growling and biting the brush.

Truthfully, it's really hard to take a seven-week-old sheltie puppy seriously; they're just really cute.

Now, can you trace any current behavior problems to the incidents you recalled?

What would you do differently today?

In Noël's case above, I did manage to take him seriously, despite his considerable cuteness. He got a severe growl and scruff grab. He's never made a fuss about being brushed since.

BATTERED OWNER SYNDROME

"But, he only did it *once. . . .*" "It was really my fault. I know he gets really agitated sometimes, so I shouldn't have . . ." "Oh, he doesn't really mean it. He'd never really hurt me. . . ."

No, this is not an excerpt from a TV talk show transcript. We're talking about *dogs.* But it sure sounds a lot like battered wife syndrome, doesn't it? In recent years, we've learned a lot about domestic abuse. We've been collectively appalled at the level of denial in battering families. We've shaken our heads and wondered: Why does she put up with this?

There is something akin to a battered owner syndrome. Owners of aggressive dogs have a hard time accepting that the dog has a problem. Owners are living with dogs who growl at them. Some owners are living with dogs who actually *bite* them.

Psychotherapists who treat battered women have to break through a massive wall of denial. Treating canine aggression is a lot like that.

Most owners don't intentionally mislead. They really have blocked the problem out or minimized it. Students become irate when I tell them their dog's behavior is *not normal.* "But," they tell me, "she's only six months old. She's just a puppy!" All the more reason to be alarmed. They think she'll "outgrow" it. No, she won't. At six months, we may still be able to do something about it.

Your dog is not allowed to growl at you. Period. (We're not talking about playtime. Although games that induce growling are bad news. Find a new game; like hide-and-seek.) A snarl is even worse; it's really a bite that didn't connect. Your dog is not permitted to show that kind of disrespect toward humans.

It's unfortunate, but some humans actually like that sort of thing. A young man approached me recently about training for his dog. He was disappointed in his young shepherd because, as he put it, "The dog isn't mean enough!" Good grief.

A dog who barks when strangers come around is doing just fine. Most dogs do this because they are territorial. Like their wolf relatives, most dogs are wary of strangers. They make great burglar alarms. A dog who bites strangers is more dangerous than a loaded gun. At least a gun doesn't just fire itself; someone has to pick it up and use it. An aggressive dog can fire himself. Meanness is *not* a desirable canine trait. Nor is it a normal one.

Fortunately, most owners really don't want a dog that bites. Back to the man with the young German shepherd. Realistically, not many people will be anxious to force their way into his yard when there's a German shepherd there. Although criminals are generally a stupid lot, even they know to respect these dogs. Check the classifieds in your local paper. You'll probably find that unscrupulous breeders are actually breeding for meanness. "Bred for protection!" "Both parents very aggressive!" No wonder there are over a million dog bites every year in the United States.

The good news is, aggressive dogs can be helped. But only if the owner acknowledges there is a problem.

Wee Willie, the Tiny Terrorist

Willie and his owner missed the first night of obedience class. The second week, they arrived early. Willie, a five-month-old Chihuahua, was being carried by his owner. She cradled him, just like a human infant. Well, okay. That's not so unusual with little dogs. The owner introduced herself and explained that she wanted to talk to me about a problem she was having with Willie. Seems he wasn't housebroken yet. But Willie had a bigger problem. Should any human or dog get within four feet of Willie-and-Mommy (they are one symbiotic unit), he growled, snarled, and attempted to bite.

Willie-and-Mommy refused to consider crate training for housebreaking. No way. They lived in a condo, and she was trying every commercial housebreaking product on the market with no success. Not that surprising.

The owner was offended when I suggested Willie had an aggression problem. At five months, this was serious stuff. When I suggested some private training, she became convinced that I was running some sort of a moneymaking scheme. Oh, yeah. What trainer wouldn't be just dying to work with Willie-and-Mommy?

I had grave doubts about Mommy's ability to control Willie, and about the safety of the other dogs in the group. She was required to work him at a distance from the other students. I needn't have worried. She had no intention of actually placing the dog on the ground. At my urging, she eventually put him down. She gave his leash a little tug, in an attempt at a heel. Willie did not care for this and gave a yelp. That was the end of Willie's training. Willie-and-Mommy had accomplished what they set out to do. They proved that obedience school was pointless. They proved unequivocally that the trainer was wrong. Willie-and-Mommy won. Neither one of them has to try to change.

The other students were glad Willie-and-Mommy had left the group. The owner made them uneasy. What went wrong? Well, from the history provided, Willie was the product of yet another reckless backyard breeding. Some owners of purebred dogs breed them each and every time the female comes into season. They do it to sell puppies. No thought is given to the health and temperament problems passed along to future generations. To make matters worse, Willie's owner had some pretty serious problems herself. She refused to accept reality about Willie's problems. She came across as an angry, unhappy person. It's sad for both of them. Whatever suggestion I made, she had good reasons why it was impossible. On some level, she wants things to stay the way they are. And they will. Or they will get worse. Sooner or later, Willie's fate will be out of her hands; animal control will step in and take him away. In the meantime, Willie isn't having much fun. He's learning to dislike people and other dogs.

Lucky Mikey

We can compare Willie's story with that of Mikey, a doxie. Mikey, too, was the product of an irresponsible breeding operation. By five months, Mikey was showing the same behaviors. By eight months, he had delivered two actual bites.

Mikey was luckier than Willie. Mikey had another type of owner. Nancy was a levelheaded, intelligent woman. She knew this behavior was serious and took my advice about private training. First, she had to establish leadership over the dog. She started teaching him basic commands at home and requiring him to earn attention and affection. Her adult daughter hated it. She actively sabotaged what she perceived as cruel and unusual punishment. She had a dozen excuses for Mikey's aggression: "The plumber shouldn't have had a hat on; Mikey hates hats. . . ." One day, Nancy decided to set limits on her daughter, just as she had with Mikey. She told her on no uncertain terms that this was IT. If Mikey's behavior did not change, she would have no option but to have him euthanized. So the daughter could either join the program and help her work with the dog, or start saying her good-byes.

Strong stuff, but wonderfully healthy. Nancy was in touch with reality. Mikey was on Tough Love. What Nancy discovered was that certain situations were high-risk for Mikey. He had not been properly socialized as a puppy, and was fearful of new people and strange things. She also learned to read Mikey and recognize when he was getting stressed. That was time to get him working. Mikey growled? Time for a sit-stay. If Nancy tried to use a strong correction when Mikey behaved aggressively, Mikey showed no reservations about biting his owner. He's got real problems. Luckily, he likes to work. Refocusing him brings down his anxiety levels almost instantly. They have a lot more work ahead of them. But we can feel more optimistic about Mikey than about Willie. They both had a poor start, but Mikey's owner is making all the difference in how the story ends.

THE PROTEST MOVEMENT

Okay, you've tried to teach your dog some obedience. You really liked the long down-stay idea. But when you try to place your dog, he gives you a deep, guttural growl, or snaps, or maybe even bites. He is protesting. This is common with dominant dogs. Remember, they are our Alpha Wanna-bes. Virtually all dogs try this nonsense at some point in their lives. If it is corrected swiftly and sternly in puppyhood, it doesn't recur in most dogs. But maybe someone else raised your pup or you didn't have this book. Now you have a dog you can't teach fundamental commands. What's a good owner to do?

These dogs really worry me. That kind of disrespect toward humans is bad news. Of course, you have had the dog spayed or neutered by now. That will help more than you can imagine. There is no reason not to get that dog fixed. You certainly cannot breed a dog with that kind of aggression.

While protest terrorism is commonly a display of dominance, we sometimes see it in dogs who are excessively high in defense drive. All dogs have a balance of several basic drives, including defense. Some dogs have too much defensiveness in them and they are dangerous. They're dangerous because, no matter how tough they are, they are driven by *fear*. High-defense-drive dogs are misreading the environment; they perceive threats where none exist. They feel they have an absolute right to defend themselves against everything, including you. How are these guys different from the scared little Missys and Wednesdays you read about earlier? Missy and Wednesday were undersocialized as puppies and didn't learn much about the Big World. They tried to avoid the unknown but responded nicely once they had a chance to investigate. When evaluating a timid dog, I always look for recovery time. Take, for example, the dog who skittered away from me and hid behind her owner, but approached me after a few seconds to observe that I meant no harm. We can be very optimistic about that dog; she was undersocialized but her temperament is basically sound. The high-defense-drive dog doesn't really recover. Each and every time you attempt to place the dog in a sit, he growls or tries to bite. Remember Robby, the aggressive rottie? Robby was scared of his own shadow, but he was not aggressive toward his own pack members, human or canine. The truly defensive dog is aggressive toward anyone who tries to dominate him, including family members.

It's also easy to interpret defensiveness as dominance. How

can you tell if your dog is simply high in the will to power, as opposed to defense? Sane dominant dogs respond beautifully to a strong show of force from you. They respect it. They even appreciate it. They train easily, once the pecking order has been established in your favor. They bond very deeply to the one they perceive as highest-ranking. Highly defensive dogs perceive a strong correction as a declaration of war. Owners of these dogs set up elaborate rules: Don't bother Rover when he's eating. Don't try to get past Rover when he's sleeping. Don't attempt to take Rover's toy away. . . . Rover rules with an iron paw. Some owners concoct rituals involving bribes. "Well, after dinner, I have to give Rover a hot dog so I can pick up his food dish." You cannot live that way! But isn't it easier to just let sleeping dogs lie? No, it isn't. It's creating the unhealthiest possible relationship with the dog. And, sooner or later, someone is going to forget one of the rules. Maybe one of your kids, maybe one of the neighbor's kids will forget about not touching Rover's priceless tennis ball and a disaster will happen. Does any of this sound like your dog? I hope not.

Excessively high defense drive is something the dog inherited. He didn't learn it. Owners of these dogs often assume they were abused by previous owners. It's possible, but it didn't cause the aggression. Excessive fearfulness in dogs is more often caused by a *lack* of early handling during the critical stages of puppyhood. Normal, balanced dogs recover nicely once in a good home. The dog has a phenomenal capacity to forgive and forget. If you're wondering whether you have one of these dogs, here's the test: Does the dog respond to you normally most of the time? For example, there is the dog who insists on growling each and every time you approach her food dish, but learns to sit on command, because it please you. Compare this to the dog who tries to bite each time the owner attempts to place her in a sit, and growls menacingly when the owner steps too close when she is napping. The first dog needs to learn respect for humans. The second dog is nuts.

The real litmus test will come when you correct the dog for an act of terrorism. Again, the dominant but stable dog will respond to a good, sound correction with a show of respect. Sometimes body language will help you figure out what you've got. Defensive dogs may act like bullies, snarling, snapping and trying to bite, but they can throw you some fear signals at the same time. Watch the ears and tail carefully. A truly dominant dog putting on a big display uses a dominant posture.

How do you get a protester to stop protesting? If you have been working with your dog in obedience and behaving like a proper Alpha and the dog is still threatening you, it's a good time to seek out a professional trainer. Try to locate someone who specializes in canine aggression. Most nonprofessional obedience trainers avoid aggressive dogs. Run, don't walk from any trainer who advises you to just give the dog more TLC and attention. And stay clear of treat-training! If you can find a trainer with a background in law enforcement or Schutzhund, he or she could be a real help. They're used to dogs with attitude. They won't wilt. And if they're any good at all, their sense of timing is exquisite.

You and your coconspirator will resolve to push the dog's buttons and get him to attempt some serious aggression. You'll have an expert there to get you through it. Lest you panic and think you're being too hard on the dog, keep this maxim in mind: If you do this right, you will *never* have to do it again.

What you want the dog to learn is that aggression toward humans leads to dreadful consequences. Be generous with the growling, threatening, and general intimidation. Let the dog think he's being murdered. It's high time he realized you have power. After a strong correction place the dog in a down-stay for at least ten minutes and ignore him, to cement in the correction. If he hasn't learned a down-stay yet, tie him someplace nearby and ignore him.

If you have found a good helper, let that person be your guide as to which corrections to use.

Dominant dogs develop a whole new outlook on life after one of these sessions. The issue of who rules the pack gets resolved once and for all time. You'll have a much nicer dog. Remember, you're only doing this because nothing else worked and the dog is dangerous.

What if it doesn't work? What if the dog doesn't change one iota after such a melodramatic correction? You've got some tough choices. The dog probably is defense-driven and he probably was born that way. You really need an expert trainer to work with you. There are other correction techniques, but they are harsh and they can injure the dog and should only be resorted to under expert supervision. With enough hard work, and harsh handling, you can indeed make a dog stop doing what he's doing. But it comes at a price: you'll most likely induce a whole new set of phobias in the process. For example, the dog who bit his owner on the arm each time he tried to get the dog to heel. Two experienced trainers teamed up to work with the dog. After several horrendous months, the dog now walks at heel. But he hangs back from his handler, with his head low. He's phobic about walking at heel. He's hardly the happy, enthusiastic working dog we like to see.

THE JUDGE'S ORDERS

Congratulations! Your hard work is paying off. You're ready to give your reformed felon some freedom.

You, as reigning Alpha wolf, judge, and jury, now must set the conditions of your dog's parole. Most dogs benefit from a transition-type program; they cannot handle having too much freedom all at once.

For example, Really Tough Love will continue for two more weeks, with one modification: Fluffy will be leash-free in the house, *provided* that there are no incidents of aggression. Should Fluffy so much as throw a "hard eye" at the other dog, she will be corrected and the leash will be reattached with great flourish and melodrama. (Keep the leash handy so you can really dramatize this.)

If the two weeks of leash-free probation go smoothly, grant Fluffy another privilege, maybe restoring her ONE after dinner dog biscuit. Of course, she must sit or down for it, right?

The idea is to wean the dog gradually off the structured regimen. When the program fails, it is nearly always the result of giving the dog too much freedom, too soon. If you've done a good job with Really Tough Love, the dog knows good and well she's been in serious trouble with the supreme law of the land: Alpha Law. Don't set her up to fail by destabilizing her all at once. The one condition that should *not* be dropped is the daily obedience sessions: she really needs those.

DEBRIEFING AND REENTERING CIVILIZED SOCIETY

The goal of any successful rehabilitation program is to mainstream the former criminal back into decent society. If you have followed the program faithfully, you will have a better dog. If you followed it marginally, you'll still have a better dog. That's how powerful it is.

You should, after a few weeks of Really Tough Love and general obedience work, start to see some changes in your dog's behavior. Some will be subtle, by human standards. Call your dog over to you. When he comes (and he had better, or he'll be leashed indoors again), watch his face. Notice the look in his eyes. Does he look happy that you wanted his company? Is he looking at you with a look of interest and anticipation? A properly educated, respectful dog is excited at the prospect of being able to do something for you. Place him on a sit-stay. Keep him there for however long you see fit; you're the Alpha, it's up to you. By now he knows how to do it, and he should really want to do it. Study the look in his eyes. Nothing is more important to the dog for the moment than doing that sit-stay for his Alpha. The way he sees it, the President of the United States is in the Oval Office, just waiting to be briefed on this sit-stay. He figures if the Alpha made him sit-stay, then sit-staying must be a very important thing to do. It's not how we think, it's how dogs think. Work with that.

Does your dog seem to feel the need to be near you all the time? Is his behavior improving? Most of all, has he become a happy, willing worker in obedience?

With the real hard cases, the seriously aggressive dogs, we have to move slowly with the mainstreaming. The dog may be eligible for parole, which grants him some freedom, but subject to plenty of conditions. For example, you wonder if it's time to let the dog have freedom in the house, without benefit of a leash. Start by giving him a few minutes, several times a day, leash-free. How does he handle it? If he goes back to the same

old terrorist behavior, revoke his parole immediately. He's telling
you he isn't ready to handle that much freedom.

One client muzzled her dog Tara after a serious assault on
one of her other dogs. Three weeks into Really Tough Love and
serious obedience training, Tara was ready for parole. Tara's
muzzle was removed, but she was kept on leash. She was placed
on a down-stay and her former victim was permitted to amble
about freely. Tara held her down-stay and ignored the other dog.
She earned lavish praise from her parole officer. It took about
two more weeks before we were convinced that Tara could be
muzzle-free and leashless. Tara got the picture: One screwup,
like growling at the other dog, and it's back to the muzzle (the
canine equivalent of hard prison time). At last report, there had
been no major parole violations, although I advised the owner
that I would not leave Tara alone with the other dog, unsupervised. We can't predict how trustworthy she would be without
the Alpha present.

PAROLE CONDITIONS AND TERMS

The intensity of Really Tough Love can't last forever. Those
daily obedience rituals can get a little boring. But slacking off
is a luxury you don't have with your problem pup. Obedience
must still be a part of your lifestyle. Now that your dog knows
basic commands, it's not so difficult.

Continue tossing commands at your former terrorist whenever you happen to think about it. Put him on a sit-stay while
you're on the phone. Get him down and stayed for a few minutes each day. Don't stick to a schedule. Keep Rover guessing.
He'll be more alert than your average bored house pet. He's got
a job! Remember, we domesticated dogs in the first place to be
of service to humans. Give your dog that opportunity. The next
time Rover is snoozing in the living room, wake him up and
give him a long down-stay. It requires only minimal effort from
the human, but it means so much to the dog.

Gainful employment is always a condition of parole. Keep
that dog working! If you discover that your pooch has some
special talents, you may want to explore some of the vocational

opportunities for dogs outlined in chapter 9, "Career Opportunities for Your Canine."

PROBATION REPORT: JET

Nobody ever believes me when I tell them Jet has serious aggression problems. "No, not Jetty!" they always insist. "She's soooo well behaved." True, true. Most of the time. As long as she gets her own way. Jet never chews things that don't belong to her. She doesn't run around like a hooligan. And Jet would never, ever run away no matter what temptation might come along.

However, on the minus side are two serious bites she took out of me, and a serious attack on my little sheltie while he was sound asleep. Jet had to be placed on Really, Really Tough Love. She had to earn back her freedom. Jet's greatest strength is her working drive; she loves to do obedience. That gave me lots to work with. When she was paroled, it was with the condition that she work, full-time, giving obedience demonstrations.

When houseguests arrived, they naturally thought I was exaggerating Jet's behavior problems. I advised my friends to get into the habit of giving Jet at least one short down-stay each day. Ridiculous, they thought. She's a perfect angel. We'll give her extra treats instead.

Within a few days, one of my friends approached me to tell me Jet was getting kind of "pushy." My friend was starting to feel bullied when Jet wanted something, especially a treat. Fortunately, my friend had enough insight to start a down-stay routine with Jet, and everyone lived happily ever after.

What happened was entirely predictable. Jet was happy to have new pack members, and she wasted no time letting them know who was in charge, as she saw it. Her natural dominance could eventually have escalated into genuine aggression when her new subordinates failed to respond to her increasing demands. The down-staying short-circuited her hostile takeover. Jet got the message, loud and clear: The new human pack members outrank you. Like all dominant dogs, Jet respected the hierarchy, even if she didn't think it was entirely reasonable. Disaster averted.

So once your dog's behavior is improving nicely, start letting him earn some freedom. Go slowly. Keep the dog working. Enjoy your achievement! Rehabilitating a canine terrorist was no easy task, but you hung in there. By now you should be enjoying your dog in lots of new ways. It really has been worth it, hasn't it?

PROBATION REPORTING

Successful rehabilitation always requires continuous monitoring. At least once a week, make some notes in your Dog Log about your dog's progress. Be especially attentive to situations you know are high-risk.

Example: Jet still sometimes gives Noël the evil eye, but she has not attempted to attack him in six months. This evening, he was snoozing on the sofa and she wanted him to move: this is what precipitated her original (and nearly deadly) attack on him. She whacked at him with her paw. Then, she looked over at me, walked away from the sofa, picked up a chewy bone, and flopped down on the floor. I gave her lots of praise: "Gooood decision, Jet!"

In the above example, we can see that Jet has most definitely learned that it is not okay to kill the little dog because he is in the space she wants. She was able to reason it through, consider the consequences, and restrain herself. That was worthy of high praise. Was my presence the deciding factor? Possibly. It's the Alpha's job to keep order. I certainly would not leave them alone, unsupervised.

RECIDIVISM

Was your dog progressing beautifully and then had a relapse? Answer the following questions in your Dog Log:

- What happened?
- When and where?

- Who was involved?
- What corrective action did you take? What result?

Now, what do you think went wrong? Did the dog have too much freedom, or was this misbehavior completely new?

Don't panic. Use your Dog Log again: start taking notes and looking for patterns. And Really Tough Love is always there for you, if you need it. If the dog has a serious slipup, don't hesitate to put him back on the program.

Some dogs will have a few backsliding episodes. It's okay. Make some notes about how you *feel* about the transgression. Go ahead and vent. And know that no matter how awful the behavior, you will never be starting from square one again. If you have followed the program faithfully, you are miles ahead of where you once were. Progress from this point will be greatly accelerated. Some dogs just have to take one last stand before they decide to really commit to the program.

CHAPTER EIGHT

Multidog Households

Getting a second dog is a loving thing to do. You know now how important companionship is to your domestic wolf. Most dogs are much happier with a canine friend in their pack.

Imagine yourself in a foreign country. You don't speak the language. You know nothing of the strange culture. One day, you run into a group of friendly Americans. Wouldn't you want to spend time with them? That's how your dog feels when he encounters other dogs in the park. All dogs need some interaction with their own species.

Adding a new pack member is going to make new demands on you. Interestingly, it's usually not as bad as owners think it will be. It doesn't really double your workload. Dogs tend to do things together. If one goes outside to potty, the other will, too. You will be spending more for food, and vaccinations. There may be extra grooming required. The good news is, you have some control over this. You can adopt a dog who eats less, has an easier coat to groom, whatever you prefer.

Did you adopt your Dream Doggie? Did you always want a chocolate Lab and now you have him? Great. How about rescuing a pound puppy for dog number two? There are zillions of wonderful dogs who need good homes. Your dog won't care if his new playmate is purebred or not.

If you're still debating whether to take on the extra responsibility, rest assured it will be easier than you think. Our domestic wolves are amazingly adaptable. The new dog may very well fit right in as if she'd been there forever. You'll get the routine down in no time.

The effect on the dogs is worth it. Lethargic, bored dogs come back to life. You may even notice some vexing behavior problems drop off. It's understandable. The dog begins to lead a more natural life. He's not as lonely and anxious.

So how do you do this so it works out right? First, be certain dog number one is obedience-trained. We want his lovely manners to be copied by the new dog. And the dogs should both be spayed or neutered. Altered pets are less testy with other dogs. You cannot keep an intact male and female in the same household without unwanted puppies and possible serious injuries to the female. It's hard to keep them in the same *city* without problems, let alone the same household.

How do you go about finding the ideal companion for your dog? Do some reading about your breed or combination of breeds. Some breeds can be scrappy with other dogs, and that may be correct temperament for the breed. In general, dogs get along with other dogs. Size is not the all-important factor. If your dog is prone to rough play, don't adopt a tiny little Yorkie. Adopt a dog who will enjoy some good roughhousing. Some breeds especially appreciate the company of other dogs. A Labrador, for example, will be overjoyed to have a playmate.

Definitely adopt a dog of the opposite sex. You'll automatically eliminate a lot of potential battles. It's not a good idea to put two males or two females together unless you really know what you're doing and you understand the breed. For example, I'd think long and hard about putting two German shepherds of the same gender together. This breed is high in the will to power. Dominance is a natural trait. There could be a serious challenge. I might, however, put two same-sex shelties together without losing sleep. Fighting is just not a sheltie trait. It helps to know your breed.

PUPPIES

In general, most adults will tolerate a young (under four months) puppy in the house quite nicely. The inhibitions against serious aggression toward babies are very strong. Some dogs, like my Noël, want nothing to do with youngsters. Oh, well. If your dog is an adult female, you could have some real fun adopting a puppy. Even spayed females often retain a lot of maternal instinct. It can be very sweet and heartwarming to watch her take care of the pup. Even my Bad Girl, Jet, loves puppies. She'll tolerate endless hours of ear and tail gnawing. She keeps a sharp eye on the little one. She even lets little squirts eat out of her dish. Amazing.

The best part about adopting a puppy is that you have so little risk of a real fight. And your adult will help a lot with the pup's education. Adults show puppies where to go potty. They correct unruly youngsters who get too mouthy.

About the only real drawback to adopting a puppy is this: They grow up. Depending on the breed, the little upstart may decide to throw down a challenge to the higher-ranking dog someday. On the positive side, by that time they should be pretty well bonded and refrain from actually killing each other. Unless one of the dogs has serious psychological problems, they'll work it all out on their own. Provided, of course, they both recognize you as the Ultimate Alpha.

THE PECKING ORDER

Because the Pack Drive is so strong in our domestic dogs, they are practically obsessed with issues around social standing. The pecking order must be worked out. Then it must be reworked over and over. With some dogs, it's a daily event. With others, they may need to check things out every few hours. If you adopt a puppy, it will be reshuffled several times in a few months.

What's a good Alpha to do? Most important is to continue to be a good, firm, limit-setting Alpha. If neither of the dogs has any serious problems, your task is to just stay out of the whole thing. Owners often, with the best of intentions, set up genuine fights. It usually plays something like this: Dog number two turns into an adolescent. He's feeling his oats and challenges the Senior Dog. Growling, snarling, swatting, and rolling over and pinning ensue. Owner panics and intervenes, yanking the older dog off the pup. Now there will be real trouble. For one thing, there's unfinished business. Restraining the older dog only agitates him further. The puppy hasn't learned the valuable lesson about respecting his social superiors. You can be fairly certain the next battle will be more serious. If owner panics, dogs panic. It may very well have been all for show, maybe even a game. But when the frantic owner started acting weird and taking sides, the tone changed for the dogs.

No, as a responsible pet owner, you cannot allow your dogs to kill each other. But keep in mind the natural sociability they inherited from their lupine ancestors. It's not the nature of the dog to hate other dogs. Sometimes it's nothing more than roughhousing that sends owners over the edge. We don't like it. It's scary. It's uncivilized. Review the sections on dog fighting in chapter 7, "The Official Counterterrorism Manual."

How do you know if it's all in good fun? Are the dogs chasing each other around, wrestling? It's probably a game. Did one of the dogs snarl at the other when he got too close to the food dish? She's just educating the other dog. He had better not pull that stuff on the Alpha. But, as to subordinates, it's entirely socially correct. You must resist the urge to take sides. You *don't* know who started it. The provoking may have been going on for days. Two dogs of reasonably sound temperament will not murder each other. In fact, they won't even bite each other. Snarl, growl, smack with a paw, sure. Quite normal. But no one bites. Don't panic if you see a scratch of two. That happens.

The better you become at reading canine body language, the more relaxed you will be. You'll get to know the rituals.

Owners interfere too much. That sets up more animosity than anything else. The rule in multidog households is this: Respect their pecking order. It may make no sense to us, but it works for them. You may have expected dog number one, the older, more seasoned dog, to be dominant over the new young upstart. Maybe. Or maybe not. Did you just assume the bigger dog would rule? It happens sometimes. Dogs have their own ways of working all this out. Do you wish they could just live as social equals, and have everything be fair? Remember, there is no equality in dogdom. Dogs must have a hierarchy. Without it, they're anxious and insecure. It feels like a life-or-death matter to the dogs, no matter how silly it seems to us.

Also keep in mind that it takes time to work things out. And it's not static. The hierarchy can change and rechange many times. And we have to respect it. If one dog emerges as clearly socially superior over the other, fine. Feed dog number one first. Acknowledge their pecking order. Dog number one gets to be first for everything. We humans love underdogs. Well, that's one way to increase the probability of a real fight. The lower-ranking dog will be quite content with his position in the pack, as long as there is a strong Alpha to make him feel secure.

All training books will tell you to introduce the dogs on neutral territory. I've never done it, but it sounds like a great idea. The problem is, they'll have to be leashed if you take them to the park or other open area. Being on a leash increases any dog's territoriality and aggressiveness. They talk a lot tougher when the Alpha is holding on to them. And it disrupts the opportunity to go through a proper Sniffing Ceremony. What most books recommend is keeping the dogs on neutral turf until they begin to play. Then, you are assured, there is nothing to worry about. If only that were true.

Some dogs will tolerate another dog in the house nicely, until the moment it hits them: The other dog isn't leaving! It may take hours, days, weeks, or months for this to dawn on the dog. Especially if you've had friends over to visit with their own dogs. The dog figures this is the same deal: the dog comes over, hangs out for a while, then leaves. He's okay with that.

When I brought my Cassius home from the shelter, I did it completely wrong. I'd just driven to the mountains and back in a dreadful rainstorm. I had no intention of recruiting a volunteer to pick up Jet and spend an hour or two getting drenched in the park. My attitude was: Hey, Jet, here's the new dog, you'd better like him. Cash, being Cash, was delighted to meet his new pack. He enjoyed sniffing around his new yard for a few moments. I cavalierly left Cash and Jet together in the yard while I made a quick run to the store. I hoped for the best. When I returned, they were sniffing and wandering about, quite interested. When they came in the house, Cash helped himself to a rawhide chewy and plopped down on the sofa. "Cash, OFF!" He jumped down immediately. (And people wondered why I adopted him.) Noël, predictably, wanted nothing to do with this hundred-pound creature. Fair enough. Jet was actively curious. This was quite interesting to her. They did fine.

Two weeks later all hell broke loose. Seems Cash and Jet had a difference of opinion about who gets to go out the front door first. We had growling, snarling, snapping, and fur-grabbing. The sound effects were horrific. I didn't do much to intervene, because, frankly, there was not much I could do. Guess what? Nobody bit anybody. They had several more battles in the next few weeks. They worked it out on their own. Jet emerged as dominant over Cassius (big surprise). Amazingly, Noël also outranked Cash. Imagine the scene: a nine-year-old, thirty-five-pound sheltie, standing on the corner of my bed, snarling at the hundred-twenty-pound German shepherd. Cash played it to the hilt. He'd stand in the hallway, ears plastered to his head, *whining*. More than once, I had to provide Cassius with an escort into the bedroom so he could get safely past the snarling sheltie. This is another reason to adopt a second dog: You will add more hilarity into your life. I think Cash knew he could put Noël's entire head in his mouth. Cash was just a good-natured boy, and willing to show the respect that the Senior Dog deserved.

When Cash turned three (at last), approaching something akin to maturity, things changed in our pack. He and Jet had another of their many squabbles outside. I watched in amazement as Cassius finally rolled Jet over and pinned her. She *hated* it. But she knew the rules. She'd been kicked down a notch in the pecking order. In true wolf-pack fashion, she started doing Dominant Dog Swaggering and using the paw-on-the-back routine on Noël. Unfortunately, he's made of pretty stern stuff, and he failed to back down quickly enough sometimes.

For all of their ferocious, semifake fights, Jetty took it very hard when Cash died. They'd been side by side for three years. He died at home, peacefully. I'm thankful for that. Jet knows he won't be coming home again. After he died, she went into a deep dog depression. She curled up on the sofa and shut down. She wouldn't eat. She wouldn't bark at strangers. She had a broken heart. We had our own little wake for Cassius. I let Jet sniff his collar. Her head dropped low, and she looked so sad. That's how we got Thunder-puppy. He joined the pack when he was seven weeks old. He was named Silver Wolf's Angels' Thunder, in Cash's honor. He was sent to us when the angels became outraged at Cash's being taken away from us too soon. He's having an easier time with Jet. She likes puppies. Her interest in him brought her out of her grief. She's a responsible dog, after all. She couldn't very well let this infant run around unsupervised. Thunder knows his place in the pack. Jet and Noël quickly instructed him as to the corporate hierarchy. He's properly respectful. So far. We can't predict what upheavals we may all face as Thunder matures and discovers he's a German shepherd. Jet housebroke Thunder with only minimal assistance from me. She showed him what was expected of him. She's amazingly tolerant of his puppy antics. Of course, we can never replace our beloved Cashie. But the pack seems much more content now.

So please be sensitive to how much a canine companion can mean to your dog. If your schedule forces you to leave your dog alone many hours each day, it's worthy of consideration. True, your vet bill for things like shots will double. But shots are pretty cheap anyway. Your dog food bill will increase. But the fun will increase exponentially. And your dog will be much happier and healthier. Pack life is natural for a dog. He'll be more alert with a competitor.

My dogs are required to sit for everything. On day one for Thunder in our pack, he watched Jet and Noël run into the kitchen after supper for their after-dinner dog biscuits. On day two, *Thunder* ran into the kitchen and sat up perfectly straight, looking at me. He'd learned the rule, just by watching the adult dogs. Dogs often work sharper in obedience when they have companion dogs in the house. They compete. Of course, if you adopt a younger dog, he'll learn all of your dog's bad habits as well. This is a good reason to train your dog before adopting dog number two.

FINDING YOURSELF RINGSIDE

Seeing your two or more beloved pets trying to kill each other is a horrifying experience. What's an owner to do? If it's a serious fight, there isn't much you can do. Some trainers advise pulling one dog off the other by the tail or hind legs. I cannot fathom how they do this. Others suggest putting the weaker dog in a submissive position, on the ground. Not recommended. You won't have a clear picture of what's really going on. Other experts advise hitting the dogs with a broom or hosing them with water (assuming you have this equipment available). Don't bother. The dogs are not feeling a thing. Try grabbing the scruff of the dog nearest you and yanking him straight up. Having his front legs off the ground disorients the dog. The fight drains out of him. It might work.

If you do suddenly find yourself ringside, try not to panic. Easier said than done, I know. Keep in mind that serious fights are rare. The same play fighting your dogs did as puppies does go on in adulthood. Complete with bloodcurdling sound effects. Much of what looks and sounds like serious fighting is posturing and ritual displays of dominance. They mostly grab fur. My shepherds still indulge in roughhousing and play fighting. There are occasional semiserious dominance displays. I'm reasonably certain they won't kill each other. Having large dogs snarling and swatting at each other in the living room is not acceptable, however. So, like a bouncer in a bar, when they get frisky, I open the door and point to the outdoors. They are quite civilized about it and walk calmly until they get to just the right spot and can resume the brawl.

Resist the urge to side with the underdog. It's too easy to assume the swaggering bully "started" it. Maybe. Some dogs who look like innocent victims actually did a lot to provoke the challenge. My little sheltie is good at this. He will spend *days* giving one of the shepherds the evil eye. Or he'll get a dog biscuit and parade around with it in his mouth for several hours. He makes quite the show of this. He'll prance around, cookie in his mouth, tail up high, daring them. It's quasisuicidal behavior, in my opinion, but he seems to enjoy it.

Owners, understandably horrified over the whole thing, frequently think the dogs have bitten each other, when all they're seeing is a scratch or two. In general, if two adult dogs have gone at it and emerge with nothing but scratches, it was *not* a serious fight. Look at the dogs' teeth! A serious fight ends with someone needing stitches, at best. These mock fights seem to be natural, good clean fun for some dogs. My shepherds are like this. My sheltie finds it appalling. Sometimes you can tell that it's all in fun: watch to see if they alternate top and bottom position. That's normal in play fights. Try not to get upset. Set some rules. Roughhousing, fake fighting, okay. As long as the dogs are outside. Frantic chase games? No problem, if they're out in their yard. Once they've worn themselves out, you can let them in to behave like civilized dogs.

If, however, your dogs are on their hind legs, pawing at each other, you could have real trouble. They're signaling that neither one is willing to submit. Hopefully, someone will have the sense to call it quits. Never separate the dogs after a battle like this. It rewards one or both of them. He got what he wanted: rid of the other dog. Crate them both for safety until you can sort things out. And serious obedience work is in order for both of them. They have to learn who the toughest wolf really is, and that the Alpha will not tolerate violence.

OFF TO A GOOD START

Be sure to do your homework before you go searching for your new addition. There are plenty of wonderful dogs waiting for a good home and canine companion. Pet stores are not always a good risk. Pet shop dogs are too often the product of what are known as puppy mills. The puppy mill is a deplorable operation. Unfortunate female dogs are confined and bred each time they come into season. The motive is pure profit. No concern is given to proper socialization of the puppies. Health and temperament problems are common in pet shop pups. And buying a dog from a pet shop contributes to irresponsible breeding.

Pet shop puppies are pretty irresistible; it may take some willpower not to give in to your kids when they spot an adorable little furball at the mall. A look at the price ought to do the trick. Pet shop dogs are frequently overpriced. Not all pet stores get their inventory from puppy mills, but in California the problem was serious enough to get the state legislature to take action. Now some pet shops are dealing only with reputable breeders and really socializing their pups. In other states, the practice goes on unabated.

Of course, there is always the local animal shelter. Shelters never seem to run out of adoptable dogs. Take your time; you want a good match. Spend some time with your prospective adoptee. Ask the staff to let you take the dog for a walk. Get to know the dog. Shelter dogs are difficult to read. They're in completely unnatural surroundings. They're often in deep grief after being dumped by their beloved owners. They're cooped up too much. It's very hard to get an accurate read on these poor guys. On the plus side, you can readily gauge the dog's reaction to other dogs because there are so many of them right there at the shelter. And the shelter will have had the vet check your new friend out, and vaccinations will be current. Some shelters will even do the spaying or neutering. Or you may be required to place a deposit that will be refunded when you provide written proof of spaying or neutering. Get it done! The shelter staff *will* follow up on this. I've talked to many shelter workers who agonize over adopting out unaltered dogs. Bring in that spay/neuter certificate and brighten up an overworked volunteer's day.

Breed rescue groups can be another source of hidden treasure. The volunteers who run these organizations are generally knowledgeable about the breed. They can be a great help in making a successful placement. You may be appalled at the staggering numbers of beautiful purebred dogs at the shelters and rescue groups. Don't think for a moment that overpopulation only affects mixed-breed dogs. I recently saw a rare Chinese crested at the pound. You can be as picky as you want to be. Do you have your heart set on a particular breed? Coat color? Age? Don't worry. You'll find your dog. Check out any good-sized municipal shelter, and that dog is sitting there, waiting. That's how bad the overpopulation problem is. Five minutes at the local pound or humane society should turn anyone into a spay/neuter fanatic.

Many dog books will try to discourage you from adopting a pound rescue. They'll tell you it's too risky—The dog may have temperament or health problems. Don't fall for this. Lots of expensive purebreds have health and temperament problems. And you'll find plenty of purebreds at the pound anyway. The shelters are bursting at the seams with wonderful, beautiful dogs. Owners give up dogs for reasons other than poor temperament. At some shelters, the staff will tell you what the owner stated as the reasons for giving up the dog. It is often sickening. "Sheds too much." "Got too big." "We're moving." This one really gets to me. I've moved ten times in as many years and I always took my dogs along. Good grief. Often the owners' complaints are about normal canine behaviors that a little training would have taken care of: "Not housebroken." "Chews things." "Digs." What was in their heads when they decided to get a dog?

So by all means earn your special place in heaven and rescue a pound puppy. Both my Jet and my Cassius were rescues. I'm just thankful they found their way to me.

HOT PICKS

As you are contemplating adding a new canine pack member, be aware that some breeds are better at getting along with their peers. By now you've done your homework and learned about dog number one. You've read the breed standard (or standards, if you have a mixed-breed). Any breed book worthy of publication will include the written standard for the breed. The standard is drafted most often for the American Kennel Club (AKC), though some breeds are registered through other registries, like the United Kennel Club (UKC). Even if you're not planning to go multidog, the breed standard is required reading for all dog owners. You'll get some valuable insights on why Fido does what he does, and what obedience tasks Fido will enjoy most. They were all bred to do *something*, after all. If you own a fancy foreign import, study the standard from the dog's country of origin. Unfortunately, many of the AKC standards are too skimpy on temperament. You'll find lots about conformation. A good breed book can be invaluable. Or talk to a reputable breeder. Any responsible breeder is committed to educating people about the breed. The good ones will answer your questions and offer information, whether you are a prospective customer or not. Good breeders are driven by a love for the breed.

If you're searching for a purebred playmate for your dog, be sure to check with your vet. The vet's office knows about upcoming litters. The vet also knows whose dogs are plagued by health problems. And her staff really knows whose dogs have to be muzzled and sedated to be examined. In short, your vet knows who is producing healthy, good-tempered dogs.

When you look at breed standards, you may be surprised to discover that belligerence with other dogs can be correct temperament for some breeds. Thus you can rule these guys out as potential companions for your dog. A feisty attitude toward other canines can be perfectly acceptable in a schnauzer, for example. In a golden retriever, it's appalling. Good goldens love everybody. When we say a "good" golden, or other breed, we mean that the dog's temperament follows the standard for the breed. When we talk about certain breeds having given traits, it presupposes that the dog in question has *correct* temperament.

So which dogs adapt well to life with another dog? Two popular retrievers, the Lab and the golden, for example, really enjoy canine companionship. They'll have a great time. To these guys, all living creatures are potential playmates. They make fabulous family pets, also. Goldens are also consistent high-scoring winners at obedience trials. Dogs are so adaptable that most can learn to live with and love a fellow canine.

Some breeds, unfortunately, were developed to fight with other dogs—for example, the much maligned "pit bull" ("pits" are actually more than one breed). If you are considering one of these breeds, get your dog from a responsible breeder. A well-bred, *properly socialized* dog can live quite harmoniously with his own kind. Responsible breeders don't breed for aggression. They handle the dogs properly. For all the current scandal around pit fighting, it's worth noting that many of these dogs have to be *trained* to attack other dogs.

Pack life is so normal for dogs, it would be impossible to compile a list of breeds that get along best with other dogs. Proper socialization is just as important as breed traits.

YOUNGER OR OLDER?

Which is better? A younger pup will adapt to the current pecking order more readily than an adult. Maybe. There are, however, benefits to bringing a mature, experienced second dog into your home. You get to avoid the whole puppy thing. Adults are relatively easy to housebreak. Many of them arrive already housebroken. The shelters are packed with fabulous, well-mannered mature dogs. If your schedule is pretty hectic, consider a mature adult and spare yourself another round of puppy antics. Dogs over the age of five years are difficult to place. The whole world wants to adopt a puppy. But puppies are a lot of work. Prospective owners also worry that an adult dog won't bond as deeply as a youngster. Not true. Adults rescued from shelters don't seem to forget. They usually bond very deeply to their rescuers. They're grateful.

So there are no hard-and-fast rules. It's a matter of personal choice. Puppy or adult? It's up to you. Provide the new fur-kid with a good education. Be a proper Alpha. You'll all have a lot more fun.

 LOOKING FOR LOVE

If you are planning to add a new canine pack member, here are some questions to help you make a good match:

- What breed or combination is your dog?
- Age?
- Sex? (spayed or neutered, of course)
- How does your dog interact with other dogs?
- What are your dog's favorite games?

Example: Bailey: Six-year-old rescued greyhound. Very gentle and well-behaved. A little timid with other large dogs, but always very polite. Bailey loves to run, so any game involving a chase is fun for him. He does not like rough play; he'll walk away from any game that gets rough.

Bailey's ideal companion: Because greyhounds are typically gentle souls, your main concern will be finding a playmate who will be gentle enough for him. Certainly, get a female. Consider rescuing another greyhound; they could play lots of chase games together and share the sofa. Other gentle breeds that love chase games include collies and shelties. The sporting breeds, like the retrievers, love to play chase, but they tend to love roughhouse play and may be too much for Bailey. Rule out the nonrunners, like bassets and pugs.

Also consider adopting a senior citizen dog; the exercise could be great for her, and Bailey's gentle manners would be a blessing. You could also adopt a much smaller dog, since Bailey isn't rough. With a sweet-tempered dog like Bailey (and most greyhounds are just like him), there are zillions of possible companions for you to choose from.

 THE CORPORATE DOG

If you have more than one dog, draw a diagram of the hierarchy. For example:

Jet
6-year-old spayed female German shepherd

Noël
9-year-old neutered male Shetland sheepdog

Cash
3-year-old neutered male German shepherd

What protocol do they use to maintain the pecking order? Jet can take toys away from the other dogs, but does not allow them to take things from her. Noël can intimidate Cash to the point that Cash will not walk past him.

Make a list of things you can do to facilitate corporate stability. Remember, no matter how bizarre it may seem to us, keeping the hierarchy stable makes for calmer, better-behaved dogs. In the above example, I can help maintain stability by feeding Jet first, training her first, generally letting her be first for everything. This will reduce her need to demonstrate her power and position to the other dogs in aggressive ways.

CHAPTER NINE

Career Opportunities for Your Canine

You have taught your dog the ABCs. You've resolved most of your dog's behavior problems by being such a good Alpha wolf. And guess what? You're having a great time! Now you're really enjoying your canine companion. And the feeling is entirely mutual. You've discovered your dog really looks forward to her obedience lessons. She's only too happy to drop and stay when you ask her to.

By educating your dog and putting yourself through Alpha School, you have developed a deeper, more rewarding relationship with your dog than you ever thought possible. Your dog is happier and more alert than ever. Now what? Continue to work obedience into your everyday routine. Never miss a chance to issue a command. Have the dog sit or down when she wants you to throw the ball. By now it's become a habit. Life is good. Are you ready to move to the next level?

APTITUDE

Remember, most recognized breeds were developed to do something. Whatever your dog's genetic heritage, you've made his life happier by educating him and giving him the opportunity to work for you. Some dogs have special talents that you may want to explore further.

No one is sure how the process of domestication actually started. Certainly our ancestors discovered the usefulness of wild wolves. We took advantage of their superior sensory skills, and we used them as sanitation engineers around the campsite. Maybe one of our cave-dwelling predecessors took an orphaned wolf pup home to play with the kids. When that pup grew up, he was just a little less shy of humans. He passed this along to his offspring through his DNA and by example. Eventually the cave dwellers discovered that wolves could not only detect and capture prey, but could turn it back toward the humans. And the herding breeds were born. Wild wolves are naturally suspicious of strangers. Some, no doubt, were more aggressive than others, standing and holding their ground while alerting the humans that an intruder was near. Hence the first guard dogs.

What special talents did your dog inherit? You can have a lot of fun finding out. There's nothing quite like seeing a dog light up when he's given the chance to do what his genes are telling him he should do. There are plenty of career opportunities available for your dog.

OBEDIENCE

Many students really get to enjoy doing obedience work with their dogs. The dog enjoys the extra attention and praise. Most of all, the dog appreciates having a job. Some breeds have a natural aptitude for obedience. The Shetland sheepdog, for example, was selectively bred to learn quickly and easily. Golden retrievers do well in obedience because the breed was developed to have a high willingness to please. Good goldens will stand on their heads if they think it will earn some praise. These are only two examples. Many, many breeds have been developed to be stars in obedience. The working and herding breeds especially enjoy obedience training. The sporting breeds, like the Labrador, are also high in trainability. They're meant to work closely with a human partner in the field.

If you're considering getting involved in obedience competition and want to put some titles on your companion, find a good local obedience club. Club members practice and prepare for trials together. It's a lot of fun. AKC competition remains limited to purebred dogs, but there are lots of other avenues. New registries are popping up all the time that sponsor their own matches. Local organizations also sponsor fun matches. Your training club may very well conduct its own matches.

Earning an obedience title should be a source of great pride to both you and your dog. Your dog will need to learn the ABCs and be competent in off-leash work. Your dog can earn titles by passing tests of increasing difficulty. Again, a good club is your best resource. The club will be current on AKC and any local rules. You'll meet lots of other committed dog owners and find new friends who share your interest.

Your dog can earn several obedience titles, under AKC rules. The C.D. title stands for Companion Dog. Your dog must heel both on and off leash; stand for examination; come when called; hold a long sit-stay and (guess what) a long down-stay.

At the next level, the C.D.X., or Companion Dog Excellent, is available to dogs who know the drop on recall, and can retrieve an article over a high jump and do a broad jump.

The most prestigious title your obedient partner can earn is the U.D., or Utility Dog. Now it gets really interesting, because this includes tests of scent discrimination. Your dog must also learn to go out and away from you on command.

Your obedience club can give you the most current specifics on each exercise. If you decide to compete in obedience trials, I wish you and your best friend the very best of luck.

HERDING

If your dog comes from one of the herding breeds, this is her idea of heaven. Some breeds retain more herding drive than others. The Border collie, for example, still lives to herd. Herding classes are popular in many areas of the country. If you're really lucky, you may even find a local club to join. Your dog can be tested for herding instinct, if you find a qualified trainer.

Though herding instinct is, to some extent, innate, dogs still need some education in this area. Your dog will need to be obedience-trained before you start her in postgraduate herding work. Even mixed-breed dogs can retain a great deal of herding drive, so don't count your combo dog out.

Does your dog like to run in circles and yap when you and the kids are playing in the yard? Does she have the nasty habit of nipping at your heels and ankles? Get that dog to herding class! She's showing drive. And she'll get a great workout. A tired dog is, after all, a good dog.

Herding trials are becoming increasingly popular in many areas. It's wonderful for the dogs and owners. The dog gets the chance to do what she was bred to do and everyone has a good time. You don't need to own a flock of sheep to have a happy sheepdog. A good club will have animals available for your dog to train on. You'll be giving your dog the chance to express herself. She'll love you for that.

AGILITY

Do you own a gazelle-dog hybrid? My Thunder is one of those. Does your dog look for an opportunity to hop or leap off of something? He just might be a natural for an agility class. This is yet another popular dog sport. The dogs get to run through an agility course, complete with hurdles to hop and tunnels to run through. They have a really good time. Many dogs excel in agility; this talent is not really breed-specific.

Your first step is to obedience-train your dog, so he will obey commands reliably. Then look for an agility trainer or club. A club will have all the equipment your dog will need. You can join for fun or enter agility competition. This is another great workout for you and your dog, and dogs really enjoy it. To the dog, it's a great game.

TRACKING

Some dogs use their noses more than others. Are you constantly finding your sofa cushions in disarray because your dog sniffed out something interesting under there? You may find that your dog particularly enjoys using her nose to find things. Does your dog sniff out things you keep trying to hide from her? Channel that tracking instinct and have some real fun.

Once again, your dog will need to know basic obedience commands before you commence her tracking career. If you have a puppy, you can teach her to use her nose in early puppyhood. You can use tidbits to lay a short, simple track for the puppy. Lead her to the track and tell her to "Find it!" She'll quickly figure out that keeping one's nose to the ground can be rewarding.

If you want to check your dog for tracking aptitude, you can lay your own track. Wait for a damp morning; moisture holds the scent better. With your dog out of sight, tromp through the damp ground, making deep tracks with your footprints. Make the track so easy and obvious even a mere human could follow it. That way you'll remember where the track is. You can even tromp through it twice, leaving double tracks. At the end of the trail, place a tidbit or favorite toy or drop a small piece of hot dog in each step. Place your dog on a long line and tell her to "Find it!" Watch what the dog does. It's perfectly all right to point to the ground and help her figure out the game. Dogs with a strong natural tracking drive will really light up. They'll know exactly what they're supposed to do. Watch their tails go crazy when they're enjoying this game. Praise the dog effusively when she finds her reward. Again, she's learning that using her nose can be a good idea.

For serious tracking, you'll want to hook up with a good trainer. It's not difficult to teach. The AKC also sponsors tracking trials. The T.D., or Tracking Dog title, and the U.D.T., Utility Dog Tracker, can both be earned in AKC competition. If you become involved in tracking, you'll be getting a good workout, too. Imagine chasing behind your dog on a thirty-foot tracking lead over hills and valleys. If you find you enjoy this sport, perhaps you and your dog can get involved in Search and Rescue (SAR). Many communities rely on civilian volunteers and their dogs to find lost children and hikers. Some SAR dogs are cadaver-trained; their job is to locate missing bodies. Other dogs are trained to search over water. SAR is a wonderful opportunity to let your dog express his natural canine instincts and contribute to your community at the same time. You may want to check with local law enforcement about getting SAR training. Or you can join a Schutzhund club. Schutzhund teaches tracking, and you'll generally find law enforcement officers involved. We'll talk more about this sport later.

PROTECTION

We've got to talk about this. Rising crime causes many dog owners to seek out protection training for their dogs. Good protection training engages your dog's natural drives in a safe manner. Unfortunately, there is a lot of dreadful training going on.

These ads are everywhere: "Don't live in fear!" What it should say is: "Live in constant fear of your own dog!" Or, to be even more accurate: "Live in Constant Fear of Plaintiffs' Attorneys!"

People ask me all the time about attack training. Never mind the fact that they can't even get the dog to sit on command. Nope. They see an ad with some guy in a bite suit and they get all excited. Oooooweeee! Let's play cops and robbers!

Very few dogs are actually suitable for attack work. You must start with a dog who is structurally sound and genetically equipped for this kind of work. Good police departments use professional buyers to act as puppy talent scouts. The German shepherds and the Belgian Malinois continue to be the favorites, although other breeds have been used successfully in law enforcement. Germany has strict breeding standards, so many police departments import German dogs. These dogs are bred and handled differently than pets. They're not inexpensive.

Not just anyone can become a police K9 handler, either. Did you know that a police officer must have at least two to five years' patrol (i.e., street work) experience before she can even apply to the K9 unit? And once dog and handler complete their training, did you think they just sort of go on about their business? According to internationally recognized expert on police dogs Bob Eden, most K9 handlers spend 40 percent of their paid time on *training*. That means half of the dog's and handler's working hours are spent on training, training, and more training. Not many of us are going to do that, are we?

SCARING THE BAD GUYS AWAY

Most dogs do this quite naturally. Like their wolf cousins, dogs are territorial. They resent intruders. They woof to announce that there is a stranger approaching their turf. The same dog may be perfectly friendly in the park, which is not his turf. Other than the barkless basenji, most dogs do a fine job of annoying burglars. Some dogs are naturally more territorial. Some are naturally more wary of strangers. Only a very few dogs are just too friendly to be efficient burglar alarms. The gorgeous Samoyed comes to mind: the last thing a Sammy wants is for people to go away. But the presence of any dog has a deterrent effect. Not all burglars have studied the breed standards.

Owners often fret because their six-month-old puppies don't bark at strangers. They aren't supposed to yet. Territoriality comes with maturity. A puppy who is barking, growling, and snarling at six months worries me. Too often, buyers ask specifically for a dog who will be a "good watchdog." They seek out dogs bred for aggression. My group classes are packed with these dogs. The owners got what they asked for. Too often, that dog with the special aptitude for guarding is too dominant, too high-drive, and too aggressive to make a suitable house pet. Leave those dogs for the expert handlers. If you are seeking one of the "guarding" breeds, go to a good breeder. Tell her you want a *pet*. Get the most docile pup you can find. The mere *sight* of a rottweiler, shepherd or Doberman is going to keep plenty of criminals away from your house. Any large dog scares people. Not all criminals are smart enough to recognize that a giant Newfoundland is one of the gentlest fellows in dogdom. To a Bad Guy, it just looks like a heck of a lot of dog to shove out of the way.

Don't discount the little dogs, either. A lot of terriers think they're rottweilers. They're feisty, scrappy, and, above all, *noisy*. That's exactly what you want, from a home security perspective. My little sheltie is an excellent guard dog. Late at night, he's the first to alert on strange noises. He misses nothing. He then dispatches his two German shepherds to go out and investigate. He has correct sheltie temperament. The breed originated on the Shetland Islands, which were sparsely populated because of the harsh climate. Strangers were a rare sight indeed. So the breed is naturally suspicious of strangers. They're quick to sound the alarm. Yet a gentler, more docile dog is hard to find. That's an ideal watchdog. And, no, neutering or spaying does not change that. That's a ridiculous myth. A neutered male does not become less territorial. Territoriality is a natural trait, inherited from the wild wolf. Neutering will decrease the urge to kill other dogs. There is where the confusion comes in. People think intact males are better guard dogs because they seem more aggressive. Not true. If these folks had been paying attention, they'd have noticed the intact male was aggressive to other canines, usually males. Other males are perceived as rivals for the bitch in heat they all desperately long for and are preoccupied with finding. Intact males are often *lousy* watchdogs. If the poor dog picks up the scent of a bitch in the air, he couldn't care less about you, your home, or your belongings. He has a one-track mind. It's obnoxious. They don't feel responsible to stick close to home and guard it. They have too much on their minds. They have to go look for that elusive bitch. And they have to kill off all the other male dogs in the world. Heaven help you if your intact male has actually bred once. He'll spend the rest of his life obsessed with doing it again. Brawling and leg lifting will be his favorite pastimes. I wouldn't count on him to guard my home.

Unspayed bitches are not a reliable lot, either. They get too preoccupied with reproduction to care about much else. They go through false pregnancies and other hormonally induced bizarreness that render them completely unfit for keeping an eye on your property. They're also high flight risks. A dog can only guard your house if she is *at* your house.

Do you want to scare Bad Guys away from your home? Get a second dog. The sound of two barking dogs will test the mettle of any criminal. He's wondering what he may be up against. There's more than one dog. How many? What are they? Adding another dog to your pack decreases your popularity with criminals.

If you want to really louse up a criminal's day, obedience-train your dog. Imagine going out for an evening stroll with your well-educated canine. Is he doing a beautiful heel? Does he sit automatically each time you stop walking? Good grief. Imagine what a potential assailant is thinking. What *else* might that dog be trained to do? Criminals hate well-trained dogs. Your well-trained dog makes street criminals suspicious of *you*. There's no way for them to be certain the dog isn't thoroughly attack-trained as well. From a dirtbag's perspective, you have too much control over your dog. A well-trained dog's devotion to his Alpha is obvious when the dog is working. Criminals don't like the way it looks. I often take Jet with me at night. While I was awaiting the arrival of my students one night, a suspicious-looking character approached. My response was to quickly put Jet through her paces. He didn't stick around. No Bad Guy is cheered by the sight of a well-trained German shepherd.

And by the way, there is no law against bluffing the Bad Guy. You spot a suspicious looking stranger? Bluff. "Take it easy, boy. No, no, it's all right. No attack! . . ." If you really want to goof Bad Guys up, teach your dog German commands. Or any foreign language you prefer. Criminals are generally a lazy bunch. They don't go out of their way to seek out a challenge. The mere presence of any dog has some deterrent effect. Even small dogs can deliver painful bites. Bad Guys know that.

You have nature's own burglar alarm. You can obedience-train your dog, to make him look like a menace to Bad Guys everywhere. You do not need an attack-trained time bomb. And please, never, ever underestimate your dog. Even little, sweet, gentle dogs have been known to come through like hurricanes when the chips were really down. Dog love is like that.

Most of us are content with a good "alarm" dog. You can encourage this natural behavior by praising your dog for appropriate barking. Some dogs are a little naive, and won't bark at strangers in your front yard. Time is often the best cure; give the dog the chance to mature.

The next level of protection is what we call a threat dog. This dog not only barks, but willingly holds his ground if an intruder tries to get past him. This requires that the dog be well socialized and supremely self confident. Fearful dogs are not good at this. You can help your dog learn. Have an accomplice come to your house wearing a funny hat or stocking cap. Dogs don't like things on our heads. Have him rattle a doorknob or window. If the dog alerts at all, praise him up. Does the dog bark at the scary stranger? Great. The accomplice should act terribly frightened of the ferocious dog and flee. You can do this once or twice with no ill effects on the dog. If you got a good response, DON'T PLAY THIS GAME ANYMORE. The dog got the idea: When scary people do suspicious things, I can chase them away and I won't be hurt. This lesson stays with the dog. He doesn't forget. You should not keep repeating this lesson; it's dangerous to keep agitating a dog. Eventually, he's going to get frustrated beyond his tolerance and need to bite.

The next level of protection is the true "man stopper." This is a dog that bites. Most people do not need or want a dog that bites humans. Such a dog is a liability. While there are many excellent protection trainers around, there are plenty of incompetents as well. You must start with a dog who is mentally stable and well socialized. If you honestly feel the need to get some serious protection training, the safest, sanest approach is to go through Schutzhund training.

SCHUTZHUND

Schutzhund is not to be confused with attack training. It's a sport that originated in Germany and has gained popularity in the United States. Schutzhund combines obedience, protection, and tracking. It is by far the safest approach to serious protection work.

Schutzhund is another excellent vocational opportunity for many dogs. The best way to learn about this sport is to find a good club. They don't advertise, so you'll have to hunt for one. Or you can call a good German shepherd breeder. This training is not the exclusive domain of shepherds, but the good shepherd people will know where the Schutzhund people are.

The advantage to joining a good club is the absence of the money factor. Private protection trainers have to pay their bills and may be under pressure to produce results for their clients. Taking shortcuts can be tempting. In a club, no one is making money; the goal is to prepare the members for competition. They can go slowly and carefully.

Schutzhund is open to all breeds, though you'll most often see shepherds, rotties and Dobes on the field. The AKC has no involvement in Schutzhund. The obedience part of Schutzhund competition is, however, similar to AKC obedience. Your dog will need to perform on- and off-leash. A temperament test is required before your dog can compete in a trial. Your dog must remain calm, stable, and obedient in a variety of situations. This reflects the strong German influence. Schutzhund judges place great weight upon a dog's temperament and attitude. They look for a happy, willing worker. In Germany, dogs are evaluated not only for conformation, but for temperament and working ability. Let's hope this becomes the norm in the United States as well.

If your interest is in tracking, Schutzhund is a good place to get your training. If you wish, you can earn a tracking title for your dog. Police dogs and handlers are often actively involved in Schutzhund activities. If you have an interest in SAR training, they can be a good resource for you. Police departments use some Schutzhund type training in preparing dogs and officers for law enforcement.

If you want to participate in the protection training, make certain you have found a good club. Get referrals, ask lots of questions. Though Schutzhund itself is sound training, the field does attract its share of crazies. Above all, observe the dogs and their handlers. Do the dogs look happy to be there? Are they having fun? Are the dogs calm and stable? Are they approachable off the protection field?

Good protection training revolves around the skill of the fake Bad Guy, known as the "helper." A good helper really knows dogs and can read a dog accurately. A good helper works with each dog as an individual, slowly building the dog's confidence. A good helper understands the dog's natural defense, prey, play, and fight drives and brings out the best in any dog. Protection, in the Schutzhund context, is perceived by the dog as a great game. It's a game the dog always gets to win. The dog's drives are safely channeled onto the tug toy or sleeve. It can take many, many months to develop a good, stable protection dog. Not many dogs have the right genetic equipment or working foundation to attain the Schutzhund title, but with a skilled helper, any dog will become more alert and confident. Good helpers don't push the dog too far too fast and traumatize him. Typically, it can easily take two years of diligent training in all three phases to earn a Schutzhund I title. No one should be in a hurry. Once you've earned a Schutzhund I, you can start getting ready for II and III.

So if you are serious about having a good protection dog, be prepared to spend many months in rigorous training. Work the obedience and tracking phases with your dog. Find a good club that will evaluate your dog honestly and doesn't cut corners. Accept that not all dogs are going to be national champions. Genes really count. Some dogs are bred specifically for Schutzhund. They're fun to watch; they seem to know intuitively what they're doing and why they're there. That doesn't mean that other dogs can't benefit from such thorough education.

If you decide to go Schutzhund with your dog, even if you don't end up with lots of titles, you will form a bond with your dog that few ever achieve. Good Schutzhund training really does bring the dog/owner bond to its highest possible level.

Now you know your dog has many vocational options open to him. We've looked at only a few. There are others. Consider flyball, a fun sport for dogs. The sporting breeds enjoy gun dog training. The sight hounds, like the aristocratic Afghan, enjoy the sport of lure coursing, and they get a great workout, too.

Perhaps your well-mannered, gentle canine friend could be put to work as a therapy dog. Check with your local hospitals and nursing homes to find the agency that certifies therapy dogs in your area. Of course, your dog will have to be thoroughly obedience-trained to be welcomed into this wonderful career.

How far you want to take your best friend's education is up to you. Just remember how important it is to your dog to have a job. You'll both enjoy life a lot more when you're working together.

 CAREER COUNSELING

What is your dog's absolutely most very favorite thing in the world to do? What is driving him? Why does he enjoy this so much? How can we channel this into a meaningful career?

Vocational profile: Thunder
• Favorite activity: chasing a tennis ball; he'll do this until he collapses.
• What is driving him: high prey drive; stamina.

- How can we channel this drive? There are numerous canine careers that tap the dog's prey drive. These including herding, the original occupation of the German shepherd dog. Thunder would also be expected to enjoy and excel at tracking and Schutzhund protection, and to be a possible candidate for Search and Rescue; flyball.

Vocational Profile: Noël

- Favorite activity: being fussed over by humans.
- Drives: incredibly high self-esteem.
- How can we channel: Noël could be an ideal candidate for therapy dog work, a career in which shelties excel due to their size and naturally good manners.

What makes your dog the happiest? Chances are, we can find a way to incorporate his favorite activity into work that the two of you can do together.

CHAPTER TEN
Dog Epilogue

 Love for Life

Does your dog have a special routine he performs when he's feeling happy and full of life? Most dogs do. They have moments in which they are just happy to be alive. For example, Thunder jumps in the air and twirls, or rolls around on his back with a toy in his mouth when he's feeling especially happy to be alive.

What little routine does your dog have? How often do you see it?

Again, you'll not only get to understand your dog's moods better, but you'll be more likely to notice when something is wrong. And perhaps some of this zest for life will rub off on you!

Can an aggressive dog really change? Can your dog learn not to wreak havoc and destruction? Yes! Absolutely. There are no guarantees in dogdom, however. What we can promise is that if you follow the program and your heart is in the right place, you will have a better dog. You may be dazed by now; it sounds like you're going to have to give up your entire life to work with

207

your dog. You don't. For a while, it's going to take an extraordinary amount of time and effort, but it won't always be that
way. Give the dog a chance; remember that serious behavior
problems—especially aggression—are usually caused by humans
by way of bad breeding or poor early handling. Don't we have
some responsibility to try to right the wrongs?

With a truly aggressive dog, your options are limited: you
cannot ethically place him in another home. If you take him to
the shelter, some kindhearted person could get hurt. That leaves
euthanasia or training. Not all dogs can be rehabilitated, but
most can improve their behavior to a significant degree. It's
especially rewarding to work with committed owners of true
problem dogs; the transformation can be remarkable for both. If
you choose to go the distance with an aggressive dog, your relationship will change in amazing ways as you two become more
like a true Alpha wolf and subordinate.

SOUL-SEARCHING

Working with a problem dog requires some genuine soul-
searching. Most training manuals offer techniques for making
the dog do something, or for making the dog stop doing something. Owners try various and sundry techniques but the dog's
behavior doesn't improve. Certainly, owners need to learn basic
handling skills, and all dogs need to learn their ABCs. It simply
isn't a matter of just finding *the* right technique. Proper dog-
handling requires a confluence of factors. Technique, believe it
or not, is the least important element in your canine education
program. Debates over technique are endless; trainers too often
get hung up on the small stuff and lose sight of the total dog/
owner relationship. Your instructor says you should ALWAYS
step out with your right foot when you issue a stay command,
but you keep using your left foot. Don't worry about it. In the
overall scheme of things, it really does not matter.

It doesn't matter because your success in educating your dog
will come from *internal* rather than external factors. In other
words, what's going on in your head and in your relationship
with the dog will determine the outcome of your training. Properly educating your dog means being centered, recognizing that

your dog is a dog, and not taking your dog's behavior quite so personally. If your heart is in the right place—meaning you truly love your dog—teaching him will be easier. Loving your dog enough to become a proper Alpha will get you farther than any special technique. Your dog will pay attention to you because he must; no dog in his right mind ignores an Alpha. He will understand what you want from him because you have learned to communicate in his own language. He will want to obey because he loves your gushing praise and desperately wants to avoid displeasing the beloved Alpha in his life. Once your bond is established, teaching commands will come naturally. Almost intuitively, you will find yourself instructing your dog in the fine art of sitting, and you'll know what to do. Good training has very little to do with whether your left foot is where it should be; it has everything to do with whether your heart is where it should be. A handler who has formed the right kind of bond with her dog has an exquisite sense of timing; she can read her dog and it comes so naturally. Watch a good handler and dog work together; notice the synchronicity. It is not an intellectual process. What you're seeing is the dog/owner bond at its best: mutual admiration and respect.

CENTERING AND DISTANCING

These are two ways you can really help your dog. Centering means keeping yourself on an even keel. Working with your dog properly requires that you feel centered. This is why you should not work your dog when you feel lousy, angry, or sick. Do whatever it takes to recenter yourself when you're feeling stressed. We're all very conscious of time and schedules. It's tempting to schedule Fido's daily lesson as if it were set in concrete. Don't do it. If you're too stressed from work and on your way out to a meeting, reschedule Fido. He's flexible. If your day has been truly dreadful, give Fido the day off and make it up to him later. He'll be okay with it. Give him a long down-stay just before bedtime. He'll still be getting educated. Most training books insist that you practice with your dog twenty or so minutes every single day or else. That misses the point. Do you think Fido doesn't know you're stressed-out and tired and do not feel like doing one more lousy sit-stay? Of course he knows, and he feels awful about it. He thinks he's the bad guy. Skipping a lesson doesn't set the dog's progress back to the degree it would be set back if you worked the poor dog when you felt terrible.

Once you've mastered the ABCs, it all gets much easier. Now all you need to do is weave obedience into your daily life. The pre-bedtime long down-stay is a great way to keep your dog grounded and focused. Offer him a sit-stay now and then; throw in a few surprise downs.

And please, do *not* work your dog after you've had a few drinks. He's a body language expert, remember? Even small amounts of alcohol affect your body language, and timing, the crucial element in working your dog, will be off. No, you need not join the Temperance Union to have a happy dog; just give Fido his lesson first, then enjoy the cocktail hour. Pound puppies and rescued dogs especially can be affected by alcohol. Many of them came from abusive homes, where drinking was a factor. The changes in body language, speech patterns, and even the smell of alcohol can really stress these dogs.

Some dogs are also very sensitive to conflict among household members. Again, we see this a lot with shelter dogs. Of course, no home is harmonious all the time, but a truly dysfunctional household is not a good place for a dog. Getting the emotional house in order for the humans will do wonders for your dog. But don't worry, dogs can handle a few emotional upheavals in their lives without sustaining permanent damage. After all, they're wolves at heart.

None of this should be taken to mean that if your life is stressful, you shouldn't have a dog. On the contrary, a dog can be a real source of comfort in anxious times. What it means, however, is that you, as a responsible, loving Alpha, must take good care of yourself. Your dog needs you.

Distancing means learning not to take your dog's behavior so personally. Remember, dogs do not act out of spite. Sometimes they chew the forbidden simply because they are dogs. They must learn not to. Other times, they feel anxious and stressed or bored. By being a proper Alpha wolf you will help your dog feel more secure. Educating him and providing career guidance will relieve the boredom. A dog who is being required to do sit- and down-stays at random has lots to think about. Just teaching your dog the ABCs will go a long way toward reducing the boredom level.

TOWARD THE FUTURE

Dogs as pets are more popular than ever. It's a reflection of the times: we really need their love and companionship. Rising crime makes their company especially valuable. What other creature has proven itself in so many ways? Researchers have measured the positive effects of keeping company with a dog. Dogs comfort and cheer people every day in hospitals and nursing homes. Dogs can learn to assume responsibility for a visually or hearing impaired owner. Some dogs can be taught to recognize when the handler is about to have a seizure and lead the handler out of harm's way. Countless courageous dogs serving in law enforcement and the military have prevented the loss of human life. Dogs know all there is to know about loyalty and devotion.

Maybe owning a dog makes us a little closer to the wild wolves. Everything we know about helping dogs and their owners comes from these magnificent wild animals. Wolves are the best dog experts in the world. It's good to know that so many people have come to care about these animals. Through your dog, you have a chance to connect with a very special creature. There is no animal that is a match for the wolf in overall intelligence, adaptability, and strength. These animals actually give and receive love and form relationships. What we appreciate in wolves and love in our dogs is their character, their basic honesty and goodness.

So love your dog. He's going to love you. He isn't sitting around reconsidering whether you would be his first choice as an owner. He is yours. As you work with your dog, try to appreciate what that means. Recognize his superior ability to be a dog. Think about the wolf connection and what that means to you. Consider your dog's genetic heritage and the specialness of his particular talents. Isn't your dog worth the effort? Rest assured that the time you spend getting to know your dog and educating him is time well spent. You will be rewarded. You'll see.

Above all else: respect.

 AT LAST!

Read through your Dog Log. How far you and your best friend have come together! Now you know how to deal with problems if they arise.

Now make a new list, for your eyes only. List each and every little thing you love about your dog. *Nothing* is too trivial or silly:

- beautiful coat
- good footwarmer
- cute burp after he slurps too much water
- cute way her tail wags furiously when she's on a sit-stay

After you have completed your list, feel free to add to it at any time, whenever you think of yet one more wonderful thing about your dog.

Now, call your dog. Read your list out loud to your dog. Say, "I love you!" Your dog knows you really mean it.

Index

Page numbers in italics indicate sidebars.

213

roots, 67–69
Round Robin Recalls, 25

Schutzhund training, 198, 203–5
Search and Rescue (SAR), 198
Siberian huskies, 120
Sight and Sound Concepts, 111
Silver Wolf Academy, 72
sit command, 23–25, 97–98
Sniffing Ceremony, 38
socialization, early, 120–22
spaying, 33, 124
  benefits of, 45
special talents, 194–95
  agility, 197
  counseling, 205–6
  herding, 196–97
  obedience, 195–96
  protection, 199–203
  tracking, 197–98
stay command, 98–100
Steinhart, Peter, 2
Superdog (Fox), 58, 64

tail wags, 42
teeth, showing, 42–43

temperament, 43–44
territorial aggression, 138–39
therapy dogs, 205
threat dogs, 202–3
Tough Love Program, 85–88
tracking training, 197–98
training. *See* obedience training
training collars, 94–95
  chain, 94
  electronic shock, 95–96
  pinch, 94–95
treat-training, 4

United Kennel Club (UKC), 190

vaccinations, 22

wait command, 116
watchdogs, 199–203
Weimaraners, 138
wolf hybrids, 118–20
wolflike appearance dogs, 120
wolves, 2
  denning instinct, 4
  dog connection, 2–3
  domestication of, 2
  pack behavior, 3–4, 63–64